Sales Training Basics

Angela Siegfried, Editor

with contributions by
Carol A. Dawson
Michelle M. Harrison
Brian W. Lambert
Renie McClay
Tim Ohai
Paul Smith

ASTD
PRESS

Alexandria, Virginia

ASTD Press is an internationally renowned source of insightful and practical information on workplace learning and performance topics, including training basics, evaluation and return-on-investment, instructional systems development, e-learning, leadership, and career development.

Ordering information: Books published by ASTD Press can be purchased by visiting ASTD's website at store.astd.org or by calling 800.628.2783 or 703.683.8100.

Library of Congress Control Number: 2009920426

ISBN-10: 1-56286-676-1
ISBN-13: 978-1-56286-676-1

ASTD Press Editorial Staff
Director: Dean Smith
Manager, ASTD Press: Jacqueline Edlund-Braun
Senior Associate Editor: Tora Estep
Senior Associate Editor: Justin Brusino
Editorial Assistant: Victoria DeVaux

Copyeditor: Christine Cotting, UpperCase Publication Services, Ltd.
Indexing and Proofreading: Abella Publishing Services, LLC
Interior Design and Production: PerfecType, Nashville, TN
Cover Design: Ana Ilieva Foreman
Cover Illustration: Leon Zernitsky, www.images.com
Printed by Versa Press, Inc., East Peoria, Illinois; www.versapress.com

Contents

About the
Training Basics Series

■ ■

ASTD's *Training Basics* series recognizes and, in some ways, celebrates the fast-paced, ever-changing reality of organizations today. Jobs, roles, and expectations change quickly. One day you might be a network administrator or a process line manager, and the next day you might be asked to train 50 employees in basic computer skills or to instruct line workers in quality processes.

Where do you turn for help? The ASTD *Training Basics* series is designed to be your one-stop solution. The series takes a minimalist approach to your learning curve dilemma and presents only the information you need to be successful. Each book in the series guides you through key aspects of training: giving presentations, making the transition to the role of trainer, designing and delivering training, and evaluating training. The books in the series also include some advanced skills such as performance and basic business proficiencies.

The ASTD *Training Basics* series is the perfect tool for training and performance professionals looking for easy-to-understand materials that will prepare nontrainers to take on a training role. In addition, this series is the perfect reference tool for any trainer's bookshelf and a quick way to hone your existing skills.

Preface

■■

Salespeople would rather sell than spend a day learning how to do it. For them, time spent in training is time wasted and money lost. However, sales training provides a catalyst for great sales performance that supports the customer. In this book, thought leaders with expertise in what it takes to help salespeople and sales managers succeed provide their insights, presenting a five-phase approach to designing, delivering, and evaluating relevant and valuable sales training. Sales training, in other words, that salespeople will want to attend because it will help them do what they do better.

Who Should Read This Book

This book is written for anyone who has occasion to teach, train, coach, or mentor sales professionals. Thus the audience for this group may include

- ▶ sales trainers
- ▶ sales learning professionals
- ▶ sales consultants
- ▶ sales managers.

A Chapter-by-Chapter Look Through the Book

Each chapter in this book is intended to increase your success in providing effective sales training. Here is a summary of the 11 chapters:

In chapter 1, "Preparing to Train the Salesforce," you'll learn why training sales professionals differs from any other kind of training. One of the biggest challenges in preparing sales training is getting the audience on board.

Chapter 2, "Partnering with the Sales Team" describes how to partner with the sales team to boost your credibility, leverage sales acumen, determine how sales team members are measured, and gain management buy-in.

Chapter 3, "Accelerating Sales Training Impact," provides the essential elements of instructional systems development, describes challenges associated with the design and development in the sales environment, and presents the five-phase Rapid Development Blueprint for Sales Training.

In chapter 4, "Phase 1: Exploring the Sales Environment," you'll learn how to explore the sales environment, describe your sales culture, define existing performance gaps, quantify business goals, explain how the team is organized, learn the five-whys approach to exploration, and get 10 tools for exploration.

In chapter 5, "Phase 2: Examining Sales Team Goals and Needs," you'll learn to respond to training requests appropriately, conduct a needs assessment, determine who needs training, identify alternatives to classroom training, target the right participants, gather data, and use a training contract.

Chapter 6, "Phase 3: Enabling Sales Team Learning," presents the definition of blended learning and explains the benefits of blended learning and how to incorporate a variety of electronic tools into your training.

In chapter 7, "Phase 4: Executing Your Value-Added Solution," you'll learn organizational skills for the classroom that really work, get inspirational ideas to motivate participants, and get some alternative approaches to delivering sales content.

Chapter 8, "Evaluating Your Impact," explains what to measure, how to define success factors, and how to calculate return-on-investment.

Chapter 9, "Making Sales Training Stick with Coaching," describes what sales coaching is, how it can help training stick, how to teach managers to be great coaches, strategies for sales coaching, and when coaching is not appropriate.

In chapter 10, "Leveraging Subject Matter Experts for Impact," you'll get advice on working with subject matters experts, including how to engage and collaborate with them and how to coach nontrainer experts to develop skills as content designers and presenters.

Finally, chapter 11, "Developing a Sales Training Brand," discusses the importance of building a sales training brand, how to create one, and how to create a sales training marketing strategy.

Look for These Icons

This book tries to make it easy for you to understand and apply its lessons. The following icons used throughout the book will help you zoom in on key points:

What's Inside This Chapter?

Each chapter opens with a summary of the topics covered in it. You can use this list to find the areas that interest you most.

Basic Rule

These rules cut to the chase. They represent important concepts and assumptions that form the foundation of a sales training effort in your organization.

Think About This

These are helpful tips for how to use the knowledge, tools, and techniques presented. They also may offer ancillary information about the topics covered in the chapter.

Noted

This icon offers other experts' perspectives and ideas on sales training.

Getting It Done

The final section of each chapter offers action steps, suggestions, additional resources, questions, or exercises to help you put what you've learned in the chapter to use in your organization.

Editor's Notebook

In addition to these icons, you will find throughout this book the "Editor's Notebook," which presents tips, advice, and relevant anecdotes from the editor of this book.

Acknowledgments

■ ■

Many people made this book possible.

A special thanks to the many training teams I've been privileged to work with over the years. You have given me opportunities that enabled me to develop this book, create sales training that works, and determine the best way to aggregate the thought leadership from content experts who can help you meet your sales goals. In addition to the many world-class sales professionals I have worked with, I am thankful to have a network of friends and colleagues that I can thank God for every day.

Thanks to Carol Dawson for her amazing knowledge of blended learning, for her friendship, and for lending an ear. Thanks to Paul Smith, a true friend and colleague who always finds the time to help. Thanks for your focus on detail and your knowledge of learning and performance. To Michelle Harrison, thank you for the many prayers you sent my way and for taking the time to share your knowledge of marketing. Thanks also to Renie McClay who has invested herself so much in helping sales trainers and sales teams succeed and continuously improve. Thank you to Tim Ohai for taking the time to share his valuable insights on sales coaching effectiveness as well as how to develop personal skills into talents and talents into wisdom. A special thank you to Brian Lambert who provided leadership, advice, and a guiding approach while organizing and improving the initial manuscript and contributed time and expertise. Your efforts not only helped me, but the sales profession as a whole.

And to my friends at Integrity Solutions, Terri O'Halloran and Steve Schmidt, thanks for sharing incredibly rich information on sales and training and helping me craft the book into its final form.

Thanks to everyone at ASTD for allowing me to grow and learn throughout this experience. Thanks to Mark Morrow, Justin Brusino, and Christine Cotting, in particular, for all of your patience and coaching! I appreciate you.

Most of all, thank you to my family (Courtney, Aaron, Mom and Dad), who supported me during this endeavor. I sincerely appreciate your patience, support, and love while offering me the life experiences that helped craft and relate the content of this book.

Angela Siegfried
February 2010

Preparing to Train
the Salesforce

Angela Siegfried

What's Inside This Chapter

In this chapter, you'll learn

- ▶ What the sales profession really entails
- ▶ The definition of world-class selling
- ▶ How to think like a true sales professional
- ▶ How to use your selling skills to sell training to company leaders and training participants.

Training salespeople is a far more difficult proposition than merely developing a course, sending an email notice, and delivering training impact between snack breaks. It entails gathering insight at both the organization and personal levels, careful consideration of content chosen and tailored to deliver the greatest wallop per second, and a sales job on your part that draws and engages your learners before, during, and after training sessions.

In preparing sales training, one of your primary challenges is your prospective participants. Let's face it. Salespeople don't take kindly to classroom time. Why? They make their living in the customer's world—meeting, talking with, listening to, and problem solving for current and future customers. Most of them don't approach the sales profession philosophically or equate classroom time with a signed contract.

Your sales training approach has to tackle this head on. Sales training is often perceived as being different from other types of training (such as customer service or management training). In fact, the principles of designing and facilitating learning are the same, but the context is different. To help, think of the content that sales team members need to know to be successful. Of course, it's probably a safe assumption that the highest priorities in sales training are (1) teaching sellers *how* to sell, and (2) teaching them about *what* they're selling. What is "sales training" within this context? Is it product training? Is it negotiation skills training? Is there more to it than that? To help you understand the differences between sales training and other types of training, consider the five content areas that, when aggregated, make sales training unique. These content areas were explored in the 2008 American Society for Training & Development (ASTD) State of Sales Training research study, which asked respondents to estimate what proportion of their total sales training content is devoted to each of five important categories:

▶ **selling skills** (soft skills, negotiation, and so forth)
▶ **product knowledge** (product features, technical training, and the like)
▶ **industry knowledge** (competition and industry)
▶ **company-specific knowledge** (back office, administrative, systems, and so forth)
▶ **sales management skills** (people management, forecasting, coaching, and the like).

The study found that the selling skills usually receive the bulk of attention, averaging more than one-third (34.5 percent) of the annual sales training content hours overall. This was followed by product training (28.3 percent). The proportion of sales training content hours devoted to industry training (10.5 percent), company-specific training (12.8 percent), and sales management training (13.9 percent) was typically at much lower levels overall.

As someone who carries the responsibility for equipping your sales team so they produce more results, your only hope of success is to create sales training that inspires and informs while it equips sales team members with the skills, knowledge, and ability to improve their core activity—driving revenue.

How Salespeople Learn

Salespeople often don't fare well in classrooms. When you think about it, it makes sense: applying formal learning approaches to all five content areas mentioned above would be a difficult task. How would you answer this question: If you had only one hour of formal (classroom) instruction with your sales team, which of the five content areas would you teach? Chances are good that you'd teach selling skills in the classroom. Although that's probably a great idea because of the face-to-face nature of skill-building requirements in the selling environment, you have to keep in mind that salespeople learn best through informal methods of instruction. In the *State of Sales Training* report, 48 percent of salespeople admit that they learn by trial and error. Informal methods of learning skills can include sharing knowledge within formal or informal mentoring/coaching relationships, engaging in trial-and-error learning, and observing other highly skilled sales professionals in the work environment. So, plan accordingly and design sales training solutions to fit how salespeople learn with a blended approach that incorporates both formal and informal learning modalities, while putting proper emphasis on all content areas.

In this chapter, we're going to take a look at the work involved in selling to help you overcome the challenges presented by how salespeople learn. Then you can begin the task of designing and delivering relevant sales training solutions where they matter most.

Noted

Learning how to sell is completely different from learning professional selling. It's like learning to be a doctor before learning how to take out an appendix. There are professional truths you must know, understand, and constantly revisit to be successful.

—Brian Lambert, PhD, director of ASTD Sales Training Drivers and coauthor of World-Class Selling: New Sales Competencies

What Is Selling Today?

Selling is no longer just about closing the deal. It isn't about checking a box and moving along to meet a sales quota. Salespeople can no longer simply sell their solutions and manage their territories without engaging others in the selling process. Salespeople now must collaborate and work with many internal departments to meet their goals—and that includes the team that trains them.

ASTD defines professional selling as the "occupation required for effectively developing, managing, enabling, and executing a mutually beneficial, interpersonal exchange of goods and/or services for equitable value." That definition requires all sales managers, salespeople, sales operations staff, and sales trainers to consider every aspect of the business, shifting from a purely tactical focus to developing an overall strategy that will produce success. That strategy involves initiatives or tasks that help sales team members develop their skills, manage their territories, and execute their sales. In short, a career in professional selling requires that a salesperson build relationships and manage the territory as if it were his or her own small business.

Editor's Notebook

By the time I became the sales, learning, and performance director I had spent 13 years in the training field and had spent time in sales. I was excited about the opportunities and confident that the salesforce would be right on my heels. It wasn't long before I realized there was a great disparity between the type of training I had done before and the type of training this salesforce needed. I interviewed key stakeholders to learn what sales training looked like to them. Everyone had strong opinions—but few were consistent. Some people believed sales training was all about how to sell—consultative selling strategies, active listening, and selling beyond price. Others held that product knowledge and technical training on systems and processes were paramount. Another group stood firm in their conviction that sales training involved all those things plus a basic knowledge of the company, its expectations, and the people they needed to meet. Elements like filling out expense reports and setting up home offices. The truth of the matter is this: You have to approach the sales profession with an understanding of what to do as well as how to do it. You have to know the "what" and the "how" to help your sales team succeed. By realizing that, I was able to incorporate these multiple opinions into a meaningful training experience.

As a training and performance professional charged with improving your organization's salesforce, you should think that way, too. How you drive results and engage your customers (the sales team) should mirror what participants gain from attending your training sessions. As you communicate and show the value of your "product," you're revealing your sales skills and expertise—the value you're offering the company in return for its investment in your training courses.

Think About This

According to the 2008 ASTD *State of Sales Training* report, 6.5 million business-to-business salespeople in the United States alone spend an average of about $400 a year on their own professional development. This equals roughly an annual investment of $2.6 billion dollars in the United States alone.

Why Are You Training?

Let's look at why you're preparing to train your salespeople. No training should be conceived and developed in a vacuum. Successful courses are built with an understanding of the environment and support the processes, tools, and activities required to respond to it. They're driven by a real or perceived need—generally at the organization level—and they should be built to respond to the organization's goals and objectives. What is more important, these courses should be relevant to the participants' identified needs. Without a fundamental understanding of the goals, objectives, and needs underlying any specific training task, you're almost certain to produce an ineffective solution.

To begin, you must understand that the overall goals of any sales training in any organization are to develop a seller's skill and to change his or her behaviors in ways that ultimately increase revenue and ensure that company goals are met. The challenge in changing the seller's behavior lies in how salespeople learn in the first place. Remember that 48 percent of salespeople in the study cited above admit that they learn by trial and error. While this may be a good thing and may show initiative, I wouldn't want my doctor or lawyer to learn that way! The success of any sales training solution lies in the learning that takes place before, during, and after the training event. Therefore, *learning isn't learning unless behavior changes*. And that behavior change may take hours, months, or years, depending on the salesperson.

And it's true that most salespeople have areas of weakness—some typical and some unique—that can be changed through appropriate training (and learning).

Noted

Learning isn't learning unless behavior changes. Period.
—Tim Ohai, president of Growth and Associates and coauthor of World-Class Selling: New Sales Competencies

Here's an example. Many salespeople who have a weekly call quota focus on the numbers and take the results as they come. They make those 20 or 30 or 40 calls simply to meet the quota, hoping to get sales in the process. As a sales trainer intent on improving the seller's performance, you want that behavior to change. You want participants to think and act differently so they can achieve the real goals. Responding to the company's goals and the apparent needs of the sales team, you might deliver a course on strategies for increasing closing ratios or ways to identify prospects, stakeholders, and actual decision makers. The result you're hoping to produce when your salespeople return to the job is that they have specific goals for productive prospecting and the skills to close more sales.

Now let's ask ourselves this: Is training truly what's needed? Or might education or development be the answer? Contrary to popular belief, there is a vast difference between educating and training. Sharing information and increasing someone's product or industry knowledge is education. Taking that knowledge and shaping it into a skill is training. The salesperson who can't answer her customer's questions about the new ZizziWig needs product information, not four hours of training in active listening. Although many people believe that training is always the answer to every perceived need or weakness, it's not true, and using ever more scarce training resources to answer an information/knowledge deficiency is wasteful. Before you prepare a full-on training solution, be sure you understand the problem as fully as you can.

Despite these differences, there is a place where knowledge transfer and training join forces. It's in the application of what one knows to what one does. Much of the U.S. educational system is based on the premise that knowledge is power. We choose to believe that if you teach people information, they'll hear it, understand it, and apply it. But information is static and knowledge isn't powerful until it's used. We all understand that people need knowledge—lots of it. But they also need a process that helps them develop new habits, attitudes, and skills, and a process that supports new behaviors that are being formed. These processes, which meld information sharing with application, are what sales training is all about!

Selling is an active occupation, involving planning, tactics, and interpersonal skill. Although your salespeople need knowledge about products, new technology, and operating procedures, above all else they need to know how to sell, how to change their behaviors, and how to develop processes for asking the right questions, hearing and understanding the answers, defining customers' needs, overcoming objections, and closing the deal. It's in the training room that they get the first opportunity to begin making changes in the way they approach their jobs.

Sales Competencies

Although every company has unique goals and every salesperson has unique strengths and weaknesses, some skills are common to all great salespeople. These skills are well defined through evidence-based research, such as ASTD's 2008 World-Class Sales Competency Study, which developed a *competency model* for the sales profession (ASTD, 2009).

There are several ways in which a competency model can be developed. ASTD purposefully involved experts from around the world to ensure the model's applicability in multinational organizations. ASTD also created a model that assumes an outputs-driven stance, which focuses attention on the outputs, or desired results, of the sales profession. Outputs are what successful performers produce or provide as a service to others. Because professional selling is very results focused, the outputs-driven approach makes sense.

What Is a Competency?

The dictionary defines a competency as a requisite skill, ability, or quality. ASTD defines it as a requisite behavior for job success. Competencies roll up into areas of expertise (the specialized knowledge and skills a job requires) and roles (groupings of targeted competencies). Taken together, these combine to form a competency model.

The ASTD model (figure 1-1) was intentionally designed to be occupation specific and to focus on the profession-wide view, which gives the model several advantages for organizations:

▶ Competencies are defined in the occupation's language.

▶ The model is descriptive of an entire occupation, not just a niche or a specialty.

▶ It incorporates expert input that is broadly representative.

▶ The results are easier to defend in court.

▶ The model can be adapted or customized to specific organizational needs.

Figure 1-1. The ASTD World-Class Sales Competency Model

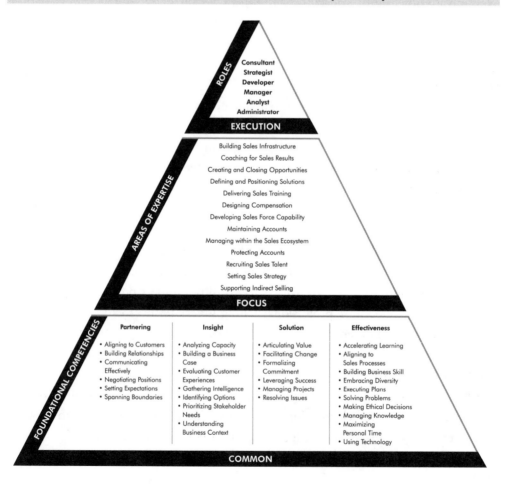

In a 2008 report, *Selling with Competence: How Sales Teams Succeed*, the ASTD Sales Development and Performance Advisory Team found that both salespeople and sales educators agreed on the five core skill sets for people working in sales:

1. asking effective or productive questions of customers
2. becoming a better listener
3. selling with the customer's best interest in mind
4. making ethical decisions
5. leveraging sales approaches that are adaptable from one situation to another (p. 14).

Think About This

Considering the five critical sales training skills defined in ASTD's *Selling with Competence* report, only 39 percent of salespeople and 72 percent of sales instructors believed that all of those skills are always covered.

As a sales trainer, one of your challenges is to ensure that attention to each of these critical competencies is evident in every aspect of your content and that you are equipping participants with the skills they need to partner with customers, gain and share insight, craft effective solutions, and maintain personal effectiveness. Just be prepared for this related challenge: Because many people holding sales leadership positions in companies around the world once were salespeople themselves, you'll probably have to defend your attention to and concern for those competencies against sales management criticism. It's likely that they were thrown a set of keys and a product handbook, given a quick slap on the back, and told to "go sell." Your leaders need to be informed about the importance of these aspects of the sales profession. However, you may find much support for these competencies—you should be prepared for both situations.

Basic Rule

Always create sales training with the salesperson in mind and, more important, with the salesperson's customers in mind.

Editor's Notebook

My husband Aaron was raised on a South Dakota farm. After studying agriculture engineering, he decided to leave the family business and go into sales. He sold large equipment—combines, tractors, and skid loaders—to farm implement/equipment dealers. He liked talking about farming, which he knew and loved, and he was good at selling. He was driven by the relationships he formed, the challenge of overcoming roadblocks, the thrill of closing the deal, and the freedom from office tedium that his work provided. When you boil it down, Aaron is a typical salesperson who loves to sell what he's selling. All in all, he's typical of the people we would like to train every day! I remember soon after I took on my sales training role, I came home excited about possibilities in our new-hire sales curriculum and poured out the endless details for Aaron. He listened patiently, encouraged my enthusiasm, and then told me plainly that no salesperson was going to spend that much time in a classroom. He told me how he'd hated training, spending the time in the classroom instead of thinking about the people he should be calling and the deals he could be closing. He chided me for thinking more like an instructor than a salesperson, and he encouraged me to look at every minute as a valuable resource that salespeople don't like to squander.

It wasn't what I was expecting from him at the time, but it was valuable insight. And that night I resolved to think and act like a salesperson instead of an instructor.

Think About This

In the opinion of 81 percent of salespeople surveyed for ASTD's 2008 World-Class Sales Competency Study, sales skills training—that is, content such as questioning techniques and methods of building relationships—is the only type of training that should be covered more frequently than the current sales skills training they receive. This content area (sales skills) was more requested than any other content area, including product training, industry training, company-specific training, and sales management training.

To Train a Salesperson, Think Like a Salesperson

Remember how salespeople learn. They like informal trial-and-error learning. So they demand more information, more hands-on learning, and a much more stimulating environment to hold their attention in a classroom setting. As you probably know, most salespeople have type-A personalities, with short attention spans and a strong drive for results. As learners, they have to know what's in it for them if they invest their robust energies in training. To get them in the seats and keep them from constantly checking their phones, email, and text messages, you need to establish a relationship of relevancy. You have to think the way they do, with a focus on the outcome, the benefit, the takeaway. You constantly must show how your training will make them better at selling. Will you teach them stronger communication skills, better negotiation methods? Don't emphasize the process; stress the outcomes.

To create successful and meaningful programs you also need understanding and buy-in from company leadership. Encourage your management stakeholders to attend the trainings you deliver so they begin to understand what and how sales training is contributing to the company's ongoing success and so they continue to support your efforts with the needed resources.

You and your training team, in thinking like salespeople, must sell your courses to stakeholders and potential participants. Remember when you're selling, you're engaging in a dialogue. Someone is selling, someone is buying. Without both parties involved, nothing of value is changing hands. See your organizational champions and your training participants as your buyers. Find ways to get them invested in the game. That's the only way they'll be open to changing their behaviors in line with your suggestions and help.

Here are four elements that are crucial to shaping a successful sales training program:

1. **Know your company goals and design everything with the goals in mind.** Every aspect of your training—from design to implementation—must tie to the goals of the company. If you don't have a comfortable working knowledge of those goals, discover them first. Then evaluate existing and potential offerings against them.

2. **Determine the impact to the company's top line.** Clearly define what your training programs will contribute to the company. Will the courses you deliver drive greater sales that increase overall revenue? Will your courses ensure employee retention? Will your classes increase the number of new sales or new customers? Will your training help the sales reps relate better to their customers, in turn strengthening and lengthening relationships? When you've identified all the positive results that training will

produce, compile an executive summary that you can share with your leadership team. It's all part of making the case for your services, and it builds your credibility and draws executive buy-in.

3. **Consult, question, and engage your stakeholders.** Your sales team members are some of your greatest resources, so connect with them often. Build rapport and create a network you can turn to for the insight you need to enhance your training. Create a plan to talk with as many stakeholders as possible. Learn their needs and concerns so you can design responsive programs. Salespeople want to know that time they'll invest in training will be well spent, and, because they're action-oriented, they'll want to have a hand in directing the course content. Engage them with a quick questionnaire or survey that asks for their input—and pay attention to the responses.

4. **Market your programs' successes.** The best way to increase awareness of your sales training programs and enhance their credibility among members of the sales team is to showcase your courses both externally and internally. Get testimonials from participants who've made gains applying the learning. Use your company communication tools to get the word out and share the successes. Congratulate and recognize successful participants in the local newspaper or office newsletter/blog. Compete for awards that local organizations sponsor. Are there workplace learning and performance awards or recognitions for coaching and mentoring available in your community? Publicize any form of recognition in your training marketing materials to pique interest and increase excitement among participants.

Diligence in implementing those four elements will pay off. Luckily for you these four elements are covered in this book.

Getting It Done

By answering the questions below, you'll be able to develop the direction for your courses and align your training goals with the goals and needs of your organization and its sales team. Most important, you'll be able to define the balance of content (product, sales skills, technology) that creates meaningful training and helps develop competent sales professionals.

1. What is the goal of your sales training? Are you trying to change sales-people's behaviors? (If so, training is the appropriate process.) Or are you trying to provide them with information they need to do their jobs more efficiently? (If so, simple knowledge transfer and education is the right approach.)
2. What do your learners expect to get from your course?
3. What does the leadership team expect salespeople to know when they leave your sessions?
4. Are your expectations different from theirs?
5. What percent of your sales training is focused on
    a. product
    b. technology
    c. selling skills?
6. Is your content tied to the goals of your department/territory/organization?
7. If there were one aspect or element of the existing sales content that you could change, what would it be?

In this chapter, you've learned ways to start thinking like a sales professional. Answer these questions to develop along those lines:

1. What are your company's goals?
2. How do your courses and programs support those goals?
3. How would you complete the following statement? Because of [*name of course*] training course, the impact on the company will be _____.
4. In what ways can you consult, question, and engage your salespeople?
5. What is one way you can market your training right now?

2

Partnering with the Sales Team

Brian W. Lambert

What's Inside This Chapter

In this chapter, you'll learn

▶ How to boost your personal credibility
▶ How to leverage sales acumen
▶ How to gain management buy-in.

What would you do if you found out your sales team members believe their personal training needs have changed and the sales training content delivered hasn't evolved to keep pace with those changing needs? Would you change your approach?

According to the 2008 ASTD *State of Sales Training* research study conducted with sales team members (sales managers and salespeople), most sales training doesn't adequately address their needs. According to this research, most sales team members agree that foundational selling skills (that is, presentation skills, objection handling, questioning skills, and so forth) are still considered important; however, higher-level skills such as problem solving, ethical decision making, business acumen, and listening are considered more crucial. Unfortunately, this same research found that most sales teams struggle to translate content requests into actual course material. This is especially troubling given the fact that more than 65 percent of all sales training decisions come from the sales management team.

The key is to stay relevant to your sales team members.

Basic Rule

If you can't find a way to be relevant, you won't provide value. If you don't provide value, you won't be a go-to resource in the eyes of your sales team members.

Why Should the Sales Team Care?

The most effective sales trainer has credibility in the eyes of the sales team. Although many people believe this type of credibility can come only from previous selling experience, I challenge this thinking. (If you doubt that, read chapter 9 and see if you don't agree with me.) As a learning and development professional, you can have the ability to engineer the right learning solutions for your company, no matter where you sit on the organization chart—you must, however, be relevant.

Credibility is not just given; it's earned. Many sales trainers miss this important point and believe that their job title should bring instant credibility. Unfortunately, your job title will get you only so far. The fastest way to gain credibility is to help the sales team improve performance! Think about it: Salespeople work hard to increase their personal credibility in the eyes of customers and prospects. As a result, they aren't prone to cutting anyone any slack when it comes to one of the most important questions they face each and every day from customers—"Hey, Salesperson, what's in it for me?" By living in a world where customers require a clear return on their investment, sales team members are asked that crucial question almost hourly. So they're likely to ask the same thing of you. If you're looking for some more credibility, you need to be able to answer the question from the sales team member's perspective—"Why should I care about what you have to offer?"

Think About This

Can you answer this critical question: Why should sales team members attend your class, be receptive to your coaching, or spend time in training instead of talking with customers? What's in it for them?

The key to answering these questions is business acumen. Business acumen is one of the most crucial skills learning and development professionals can have. They understand and embrace the "What's in it for me?" questions they receive. Great sales trainers build credibility by clearly tying their learning solutions to business outcomes.

A Sales Acumen Primer

Your business case for a sales training solution should always address the skills and performance drivers that help sales executives achieve their most important goals. To do this, you need to understand how business acumen is applied as "sales acumen." There are several key sales concepts that require your understanding:

- **Sales process**—A sales process is a series of customer-centric steps and tasks required of salespeople in effective selling. The most successful sales processes must create value for both customers and the sales organization. A typical example might include various tasks such as prospecting, qualifying, fact finding, proposing, presenting, and closing. Usually represented by a phrase like "the nine steps of the customer relationship," the sales process is often standardized across the sales team.
- **Sales pipeline**—A sales pipeline (sometimes called a sales funnel) is a means to identify all sales opportunities and help the salesperson allocate selling time more effectively. It is a critical sales planning and management tool for setting priorities. It provides a method to increase attention on sales opportunities that represent the greatest reward.
- **Sales cycle**—A sales cycle is the length of time it takes for a customer to progress through the sales process from initial inquiry to the actual sale. In contrast, the buying process is a broader view that begins at the customer's need awareness and vendor identification and goes through negotiation to

final purchase. To improve sales effectiveness, the sales cycle must be closely aligned with the buying process of the target audience.

▶ **Sales forecast**—A sales forecast is a short-term prediction of pending sales by sales team members and the sales organization. The forecast provides crucial financial information for the company's senior leadership for use in administrative, manufacturing, service, and other departments. Forecasts are used to allocate resources and help manage cash flow, project investments, and other purchases.

When tying your sales training to sales acumen, ask these questions:

1. How does your training support the sales process?
2. How does your training shorten the sales cycle?
3. How does your training help with sales forecasting?

Noted

You can't teach a kid to ride a bicycle in a seminar.
—*David Sandler, Sandler Sales Training*

Think Like a Sales Executive

To be more effective and to strengthen your position as an integral part of the sales team, it's important to link your sales acumen with some thought leadership around the learning function. Why? As a sales trainer, you're often recommending strategic solutions to tactical problems. This requires you to immediately address short-term challenges (leveraging sales acumen) while engineering lasting performance (leveraging thought leadership in learning). To balance the long and short terms, you must gain a thorough understanding of the selling environment. It's time to do your homework and place yourself in the shoes of the sales executive. Visualize yourself as the vice president of sales and ask questions to gain an understanding of his or her challenges. Of course, leveraging sales acumen helps build your credibility as someone who understands the complicated world of selling, but, more important, it will help you identify ways to make a contribution. For example, to build a strong business case for a sales training solution, you need to understand what keeps most sales executives up at night. Yes, revenue and profit growth are the primary issues, but there's more than that.

Editor's Notebook

Whenever a sales manager comes to me with "I want to run training on _____," I try to figure out a way I can provide both *what he wants (the training he's asking for) and what he needs (the training that will close the performance gap). Often, those two are related, but the sales manager doesn't realize it. My job is to help him realize it by becoming a trusted partner who can engage in serious, insightful, and relevant conversations about his challenges.*

As a skilled training professional, you have a wealth of tools and techniques to address individual development requirements. When you meet with the sales management team, you can use the following questions to position yourself as a trusted partner. With an understanding of the answers to these questions, you can begin to craft sales training solutions that address important management priorities:

1. **What are the key strategies for growing the business this year?** Understanding the sales team's key strategies and priorities will help you formulate a training strategy. It will also help identify the measurable results that training needs to provide. If you can't recommend a sales training solution that ties into this question, it's probably not going to get funded.

2. **How strong are the organization's capabilities to execute these strategies?** Knowing areas of perceived strength can suggest areas of potential weakness in the sales team that can be further developed or enhanced.

3. **What are the critical issues facing the sales team and the business?** Determining which issues are most critical to sales management will help you focus attention in the right areas. Addressing the training needs associated with these factors must be a priority.

4. **How skilled is your team in executing your sales strategy?** Is the sales organization sufficiently skilled? A needs assessment will uncover skill gaps. Your role as a business consultant will be able to demonstrate the impact of a specific competency gap.

Gaining Management Buy-In

It can be challenging to compete for resources or convince sales leadership about the most appropriate course to take when addressing competency gaps. Although there is no magic formula that will convince senior management to support your training initiatives, using business terms instead of training terms will give you a head start. The next step is to become a true business partner and trusted adviser. To achieve this, it's important to meet with every business-unit leader you can to develop key relationships and learn more about their particular issues and requirements. Bring knowledge of the market, the competition, and the firm's performance. Listen and ask questions. Ask for clarification if it's needed, and make sure you let each business-unit leader know you will be back to address his or her concerns.

Editor's Notebook

Sales Leadership Concerns

Did you know the sales leadership team thinks about the following issues?

- *How important are gross margin and operating margin?*
- *How does your sales team show a return-on-investment for the product/ service it sells?*
- *How often does discounting occur? Why?*
- *What profitability measures and initiatives exist?*
- *What does the management believe is happening in regard to "selling with value" versus "selling with price"?*
- *What's the company's position in the market?*
- *Is the market growing or shrinking?*
- *Who are your major competitors?*
- *How is the salesforce winning against major competitors?*
- *How is your sales team protecting its position in the marketplace?*
- *How is the company growing its business faster than its expenses?*
- *Is the sales team retaining the most important and profitable customers?*
- *What's the sales team turnover rate? How does this compare with that of competitors?*
- *What salesperson competencies need to be improved now and in the future?*
- *What's the sales training mix? How do you deliver product knowledge, company knowledge, industry knowledge, or selling skills at each level of the sales team?*

A key way to get management buy-in is to understand how sales teams are measured. Nearly everything about a high-performing sales team is measured. For two reasons, it's important that you understand how your sales team is measured: First, it keeps your discussions relevant. For example, when conducting a ride-along with a sales team member, is it appropriate to discuss her reaction to the latest product training when she's facing a $50,000 revenue shortfall for the year in the account you're going to visit? Probably not. The sales team member has pre-call strategy to discuss, questions to formulate, and logistics to take care of in the hopes of conducting a successful call. Second, you'll gain enough knowledge over time to create a long-term strategy for driving sales performance. Although most sales training solutions are extremely shortsighted and reactive, a longer-term strategy can be accomplished by appropriately tying sales training to key performance measures over the long term.

Basic Rule

Always start your sales training initiative by thinking about your customer's customer. In other words, think about your sales team and how its members will implement your training or development initiative. Think about how the initiative will affect their interaction with their own customers and clients. If you can't picture your training solution in action with your sales team, then you may be pursuing the wrong initiative.

Getting It Done

In this chapter, we discussed ways for you to stay relevant to your sales team. To help you stay focused, here are the top 10 things you must do before or during every meeting with your sales leadership team:

1. Prepare, prepare, prepare.

    ▶ Do your homework.
    ▶ Be sure you have a clear and concise agenda.
    ▶ Have a specific goal for the meeting.

2. Build your understanding of the world in which your sales team operates.

   ▶ Identify your company's top clients.
   ▶ Understand how your sales teams are organized.
   ▶ Know the sales team's number-one goal for the year.

3. Prepare pertinent, insightful questions, and be prepared to *listen!*

   ▶ Give the management team the opportunity to provide feedback and direction to any plans, thoughts, or ideas.
   ▶ Write down important comments on paper for later review.

4. Get your head in the "sales game."

   ▶ Think speed, efficiency, low maintenance, high flexibility, rapid change, and so forth.
   ▶ Remember that your light bills don't get paid without someone selling something!
   ▶ Recall what happened the last time you were on the road with the sales team. What was it like?

5. Remember to keep it simple.

   ▶ Communicate concisely and courageously.
   ▶ Over-engineered complexity isn't a good thing—and almost everything from the training organization looks over-engineered to the sales team! Try preparing an executive summary with bulleted lists instead.

6. Focus on keeping content relevant.

   ▶ Remember that most sales managers are scared of the word "intervention"; use "training solution" or "learning solution" instead. Make sure you thoroughly understand the competencies required for sales teams to succeed.
   ▶ Help your leadership team share its understanding of the knowledge, skills, and abilities required to succeed at each level.

7. Stay focused on the positives.

   ▶ It isn't a good idea to lead a conversation with a statement like, "Your team's morale is low." Try focusing on what is working well, or what you've seen that contributes to success. If you point out areas for improvement, always offer options.

8. Understand what success looks like to your sales leadership team.

   ▶ Revenue goals, customer satisfaction, customer retention, lower turnover, and so forth.

9. Understand how to tie learning and development initiatives to sales team performance.

   ▶ Does it help them sell more, faster? Does it help in crucial conversations with the organization's C-level executives?

10. Remember to close the business!

   ▶ Ask for the order with your sales team. Ask, "When would you like to get started on this?" (By the way, that's an assumptive close.)

Accelerating Sales Training Impact

Brian W. Lambert

▪▪

What's Inside This Chapter

In this chapter, you'll learn

▶ Essential elements of instructional systems development

▶ Design and development challenges in the sales environment

▶ Five-phase Rapid Development Blueprint for Sales Training.

A ll great sales trainers have a solid approach to developing and delivering world-class sales training. Instructional systems development is based on the belief that training is most effective when it provides learners with clear statements of what they must be able to do as a result of training and how their performance will be evaluated. The program is then designed to teach the skills through hands-on practice, or performance-based instruction. There are many instructional systems development models. Among them is the ADDIE model that has proved itself again and again through the fundamental and basic processes. The name "ADDIE" represents the first letters of each of the five elements of the model: **A**nalysis, **D**esign, **D**evelopment, **I**mplementation, and **E**valuation. The intention of the model is to focus on one element at a time and then confirm that it has been completed correctly before moving to the next element.

Noted

I cannot teach anybody anything, I can only make them think.
—Socrates

Components of Instructional Systems Development

Below is a short description of each component to help you familiarize (or re-familiarize) yourself with the model. For more extensive information on the ADDIE model, see ASTD *Infoline,* No. 259706, "Basics of Instructional Systems Development."

Analysis

The first element of the ADDIE model looks at the who, what, where, when, why, and by whom of the design process. It includes analysis of

- ▶ needs, both current and future
- ▶ goals and objectives
- ▶ trainees' profiles
- ▶ delivery systems
- ▶ resources and constraints.

Design

This is the planning stage. It consists of

- ▶ developing instructional objectives
- ▶ identifying the learning steps required
- ▶ developing tests to show mastery of tasks to be trained
- ▶ listing the entry behaviors required
- ▶ developing the sequence and structure of the course.

Basic Rule

Learning is always happening. It's a matter of whether people are learning what they should be learning, when they should be learning it, how they should be learning it, in a way that will help move them toward achieving effectiveness for corporate and personal sales goals.

Development

At this point, training materials and content are selected and developed, based on the learning objectives. This element includes the development of

▶ the instructional management plan

▶ training materials (instructor guides, agendas, reading material, audiovisual aids)

▶ training methods

▶ program evaluation materials (evaluation plan, checklists, tests, questionnaires)

▶ training documentation (trainees' records and course documentation, such as objectives, course materials, and lists of instructors).

Implementation

During this stage the course or training session is taught.

Evaluation

The final element of the ADDIE model is the ongoing process of developing and improving instructional materials, based on evaluations conducted during and after the implementation.

Design and Development Challenges in the Sales Environment

As a sales training and development professional, your role is to design, develop, and deliver sales training and development programs to help prepare every member of the sales organization to perform at his or her very best. Possessing a solid instructional systems development philosophy will go a long way to helping you overcome the many unique challenges that the sales environment can pose as you try to design and deliver sales training that your sales team appreciates.

There is no one "right way" to train and develop salespeople. In addition to individuals being unique, businesses differ in the size and scope of their sales organizations. Because of the uniqueness of individuals and organization, you'll have to take a continuous improvement approach and constantly reevaluate your training and development programs. Here are two key questions you must answer to determine the breadth and depth of your role and responsibilities:

1. Who in your business is involved in selling?
2. How can you best support them?

In answering those questions, you have to consider how your organization sells. How does it engage in the selling function in the marketplace? There are two primary sales channels your firm can employ in selling your products and services. They are *direct channels* and *indirect channels*. Direct channels include outside sellers and inside sellers who work directly for your firm. They engage the customer and are typically paid for their performance (commissions and bonuses). An example of a firm using a direct channel would be a telecommunications company selling equipment and services to consumers and companies. Indirect channels include resellers and value-added partners who represent your firm's products or services. The sales team in this channel works for a different company, not your own. An example of a firm using an indirect channel would be a manufacturer of computers who allows large retail organizations to sell its computer equipment.

Think About This

Who in your business is involved in selling? In a word, *everyone*. Everyone in the business who in some way affects the customer experience is involved in selling to some degree.

No matter which channel you're developing sales training for, you'll have to use the principles found in the ADDIE model to answer the following questions:

1. What selling competencies—knowledge, skills, and abilities—are required to successfully perform the selling functions of each functional role in the business?

2. What are the most effective and cost-effective methods for providing the training and support to the people performing each of these roles and for enabling them to perform at peak effectiveness?

With those basic questions answered, you'll also need to keep in mind the changes found within the sales profession. Over the last three decades, business professionals have experienced an accelerating rate of change in their world, their lives, and how business is conducted on the global stage. There are a number of significant trends affecting today's salespeople and sales organizations. These trends influence market conditions, buying behavior, buyer expectations, and the role of the salesperson. In addition, these trends will directly impact the content and style of sales training and development programs.

Macro Trends Affecting the Sales Organization

Some common macro trends in today's business world include globalization, competition, technology, and demographics. Each of the trends is discussed here:

▶ **Globalization**—Empowered by advancements in technology and transportation, the doors are opening for businesses to expand their reach into new markets, on a global scale.

▶ **Competition**—Sparked by globalization, and accelerated by technology, the competitive arena is being filled with more and louder voices, with greater ability and agility to respond and attack.

▶ **Technology**—Advancements in technology enable easier entry of new competitors to the market by compressing the time window on innovations and making information easily accessible for everyone.

▶ **Demographics**—It's common today to find members of three or four generations in the workplace.

Basic Rule

To design and deliver effective professional sales development programs, you first must determine how your training aligns with the business needs of your firm.

The marketplace is also forward looking and fast moving. But much of sales training and development has been static and rooted in tradition. It's important that you keep a finger on the pulse of the market so you can best prepare the people you support for future success. Within this new business environment, we are seeing a number of significant trends in buying behavior:

▶ **More buying influences involved in each sale**—In a business culture that has become more collegial, it's common for more individuals and groups to have a voice in the buying process.

▶ **Lengthening buying cycles**—With the addition of more voices to the buying process, and with tighter budgetary and process controls, increased competition, and more rapidly changing information and offerings entering the market, it's common for buying cycles to grow longer.

▶ **Greater volatility in the marketplace**—More voices in the process, more competitors in the arena, lengthening cycles, and a more rapidly changing economic environment lead to increased volatility. This means that there is an increasing chance that any given opportunity will change in shape and scope (or will go away entirely) the longer it goes unresolved.

▶ **Product homogenization**—As human beings, we have a limited ability to differentiate among choices before they all become one in our minds. When they become "all the same" in the buyer's mind, the primary differentiator becomes price.

▶ **Demand for mass customization**—The flexibility and agility afforded by technological advancement have made businesses more flexible in what they can offer. As a result, buyers expect to have what they want, the way they want it, when they want it.

▶ **Buyers replacing "vendors" with "partners"**—The salesperson used to be the purveyor of proprietary information. With information becoming ubiquitous, buyers are expecting the salesperson to serve more in the capacity of consultant helping them assess the value of an offering, not merely as a resource for information.

The Three Pathways to Sales Effectiveness

The central focus of sales training and development is supporting the mission to drive greater sales effectiveness. Brian Lambert of ASTD's Sales Training Drivers defines sales effectiveness as

The ability of customer-facing professionals to win and maintain profitable and loyal customer relationships through the most time-efficient, cost-effective, and professionally ethical means possible.

Think About This

To get off to a quick start, you must have focus and take action quickly. Your ability to accomplish the right tasks at the right time will enable you to make an impact quickly. And your ability to know where you are and (more important) what you need to accomplish next are keys to becoming a world-class sales trainer. This requires you to master the art of sales effectiveness.

In 2009, when asked by the sales effectiveness research firm CSO Insights to identify their top priorities for the coming year, sales leaders consistently rank *increasing revenues* as their number-one priority, followed closely by *increasing sales effectiveness*. In the quest for increased sales effectiveness, there are three primary pathways you can use to help elevate the performance of the sales teams you support: sales training, sales coaching, and enabling technologies.

Sales Training

Sales training is a learning and development solution that is applied to improve the individual competency of sales team members. Sales training activities can be designed to facilitate the learning and development of new and existing skills, and to improve the performance of specific sales-related tasks. Various activities are used for sales training, including classroom-based courses, on-the-job training, and business or simulation games. Audiovisual and multimedia aids—videos and CD-ROMs— also may be employed. Overall, training should result in individual learning and enhanced organizational performance.

Sales training solutions can be delivered in many ways, but generally there are two types of sales training solutions with which you should be concerned:

▶ **formal solutions**—structured (classroom) sales training programs, delivered both internally and externally

▶ **informal solutions**—unstructured learning through mentors, peers, and other resources or through interactive activities such as group discussion or role playing that promote experiential learning.

Sales Coaching

Sales coaching and managerial coaching share many similarities. Both are ongoing processes between the supervisor and the employee, both involve delivering feedback, and both have the goal of developing personnel. But being adept at traditional coaching does not necessarily prepare someone to be successful with sales team members. A sales coach must be familiar with what motivates salespeople, how to best deliver feedback to them, and when to just get out of their way. There are two types of sales coaching you should be concerned with:

▶ **formal sales coaching**—structured coaching and mentoring programs
▶ **informal sales coaching**—teaching moments that occur during the daily course of business.

Enabling Technologies

Enabling technologies are designed to support the effective deployment of your sales training and sales coaching solutions within the sales environment. Enabling technologies can help you gather data, communicate more effectively, and build in continuous reinforcement. Here are some examples:

▶ **e-learning**—technology-enabled learning systems that support self-directed learning activities
▶ **learning management systems**—technology platforms to help direct and deliver training on demand
▶ **sales knowledge management systems**—knowledge and resource repositories that can be queried for help and contributed to by members of the community
▶ **customer relationship management systems**—Many of these applications offer the ability to deliver sales resources to users on demand
▶ **other technological resources**—web resources, databases, document directories, communications devices, and a broad array of other tools.

■ ■ ■

Editor's Notebook

As a sales training and development professional, I constantly have to remind myself that I can best serve my firm when I have a clear view of the big picture, and how each role in the sales organization fits into that picture. My personal mission is to design and deliver training that leverages how salespeople learn best within the sales environment of my firm.

How well you employ the pathways of sales training, coaching, and enabling technologies will have a direct bearing on the effectiveness of your sales training initiatives.

Five-Phase Rapid Development Blueprint for Sales Training

The Rapid Development Blueprint for Sales Training (figure 3-1) was developed by ASTD as a proven process for designing, developing, and delivering effective sales training and development programs. It is based on the principles found in the ADDIE model discussed earlier. It's important to understand the Rapid Development Blueprint because it serves as the foundation for the rest of this book. Understanding it now will enable you to benefit from the remaining chapters.

Figure 3-1. Five Phases of the Rapid Development Blueprint

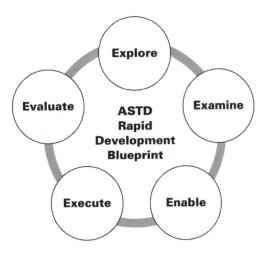

The Rapid Development Blueprint is

▶ a scalable model that serves as a process for creating targeted, effective sales training and development programs

▶ a proven set of principles and practices that can be applied with equal effectiveness whether you are developing a one-hour sales meeting or a week-long sales training program

▶ a proven process for designing and deploying sales training and development programs that support the learners.

The Rapid Development Blueprint is *not*

▶ a one-size-fits-all template for creating sales training and development programs

▶ a rigid set of standards proclaiming the Dos and Don'ts of sales training and development. The blueprint enables you to be fast moving and adaptable without getting too bogged down.

The blueprint process includes these five phases:

▶ phase 1: explore
▶ phase 2: examine
▶ phase 3: enable
▶ phase 4: execute
▶ phase 5: evaluate.

By following the blueprint's approach throughout this book, you will be following a proven, expedited process for developing effective professional sales training and development programs that support the use of best practices in workplace learning and performance. The approach can help you properly diagnose the root challenges to target for sales training and development initiatives, and help you minimize the time and money required to develop and deploy sales training and development initiatives. This blueprint also can help you determine the best methods and modalities for deploying and supporting training initiatives, and it can lead you through a development process designed to support your learners and frontline coaches.

Phase 1: Explore

The *explore* phase may be the most important phase of the Rapid Development Blueprint. It is focused on identifying the broader organizational goals and sales-specific goals that will be affected by your sales training and development solution.

More broadly focused than a needs analysis (the next phase of the blueprint), this phase will help you identify business goals; determine the business results currently being realized by the sales team; identify core competencies to be mastered in order to best support achievement of the stated goals; and identify the knowledge, skills, and abilities currently being used. By spending some time in this first phase, you'll be conducting a thorough environmental scan that encompasses the training, development, and performance issues in the sales team and synchronizing your approach with the larger corporate strategy.

The depth and breadth of your fact-finding mission will be significantly influenced by

- the resources available (human, financial, and technical)
- the lead time available before the course's due date
- the strategic importance of your training solutions to the leadership team
- the anticipated life cycle of the deployment
- other factors.

The key actions of the *explore* phase include

- qualifying and quantifying the scope of the business problem to be addressed by the training initiative
- conducting interviews and assessments
- gathering background information and supporting resources
- identifying the sales culture of your organization.

The key outcomes of the *explore* phase are

- determining the business goals to be achieved
- determining the current state of the sales environment, and the results currently being achieved
- identifying the competencies and expertise to be mastered by each role in the sales organization
- identifying the change management approach you need to take.

Chapter 4 covers this first phase of the blueprint in much more detail.

Phase 2: Examine

The second phase of the Rapid Development Blueprint is *examine*. In this phase, you take your new knowledge of the selling organization and focus it on identifying specific needs you will address through specific sales training and development solutions. In this phase, you'll focus on a robust needs analysis while examining the specific sales team challenges and responding to training requests from the sales management team.

The key actions of the *examine* phase are

- ▶ quantifying and prioritizing gaps in business goals and results
- ▶ identifying competency gaps (knowledge, skills, and abilities)
- ▶ setting the scope for the training initiative.

The key outcomes of the *examine* phase are

- ▶ assessing the individual performance gaps between where results are and where they are expected to be
- ▶ identifying the specific competencies to be addressed by the training initiative and the topics to be addressed in training
- ▶ assessing available resources to support the initiative and resources that may need to be acquired.

Chapter 5 addresses this second phase in greater detail.

Phase 3: Enable

The third phase of the blueprint is *enable*. This phase helps you bridge the needs you examined in the previous phase with the learning solutions you will execute in the next phase. In this phase, you make key choices regarding length of delivery, delivery format, and course/class design. Your choices will help determine the ultimate success (or failure) of your learning solutions, so decide wisely here. I've found that the choices I make regarding sales training program(s) are significantly influenced by the resources I have available. These resources often dictate how much flexibility I have. So a key aspect of this phase will be your ability to juggle the human, financial, and technical resources that exist in-house or are available through outsourcing.

For example, human resources are an important consideration because you will need to leverage your team to gain the success you're seeking. Additionally, you'll need to manage your team of vendors and subject matter experts (SMEs) to develop and deliver the sales training solution you envision. Another example will be the investment decisions you make. Let's face it: Sometimes you have a limited budget, and you have to juggle the learning outcomes with the enabling solution to

(1) develop and implement something of value to the sales team, and (2) do it in a way that keeps you within your budget. Sometimes you'll have to fight for more financial resources, so having a well-thought-out needs analysis (from the *examine* phase) can help you articulate the value of your approach—and gain the financial resources you need. As a final example, the technical considerations in today's learning environment must be considered. Whether you decide to use mobile learning (on smart phones, handheld devices, and the like) or you decide to use a more formal classroom setting, technology undoubtedly will have some role to play. It's in this phase where you make those decisions. Through all of the choices you make, the support of sales leadership and frontline sales management/coaches will be crucial. Therefore, you'll need to leverage the insight you gained from the previous two phases to get the job done here.

The key actions of the *enable* phase include

▶ deciding whether to buy or to build a training solution
▶ developing training programs that capture the learner's attention.

The key outcomes of the *enable* phase include

▶ having a complete sales training plan that will support the learners
▶ having a sales training program that conforms to the proven best practices for training sales professionals.

Chapter 6 discusses this third phase more extensively.

Phase 4: Execute

The fourth phase of the Rapid Development Blueprint is the *execute* phase. This is the phase in which your ultimate impact will be achieved and realized. (It will be measured and proved in the next phase, but realized here.) For this phase, you'll need to manage the actual delivery to keep the sales audience engaged and learning throughout the course. You'll leverage the design and delivery plans you made to execute flawlessly and perform well in front of the audience. In this phase, you'll leverage the resources and tools you have available to make the sales training work for your sales team, for your management team, and for you. A key aspect of the *execute* phase is also your understanding of, and ability to leverage, the power of blended learning approaches so you maximize the effectiveness and minimize the footprint of your sales training initiatives. Blended learning approaches help you balance your human, financial, and technical resources to provide a personalized learning experience through a smart blend of formal and informal learning methods.

Editor's Notebook

I often have discussions with external sales trainers who focus almost exclusively on the execute *phase of the Rapid Development Blueprint. That phase is easy to see and it "speaks the language" of the sales team—action and results. Because everyone (including the sales management team) can observe the phase in action, it's easy to focus there, start there, and even end there. In other words, it's easy for the* execute *phase to become the only phase that gets any real attention and thought. My strong advice is this: Don't fall into that trap! Be a consultant and adviser and stay true to the system's approach. It's been proved to work.*

The key actions of the *execute* phase include

▸ selecting the appropriate delivery modalities
▸ leveraging the power of blended learning to reduce the cost and increase the effectiveness of professional sales training
▸ getting prepared to be an effective facilitator
▸ getting prepared to coach learners after training and to conduct coach-the-coach sessions.

The key outcomes of the *execute* phase are

▸ having a complete sales training plan that will support both sales-wide learning plans and personal learning plans
▸ being able to deliver targeted, effective, professional development programs using methods and modalities that most effectively and cost-effectively take the training to the people
▸ being able to deliver professional sales development programs in a way that supports learners throughout the entire learning process.

Chapter 7 covers the *execute* phase in greater detail.

Phase 5: Evaluate

The fifth and final phase of the blueprint is the *evaluate* phase. This phase is extremely important because it can help you make relevant adjustments to future training and development programs and analyze the effectiveness of your personal approach with the previous four phases. In other words, this phase should help you (1) evaluate the design by identifying appropriate evaluation techniques and applying them, and (2) evaluate and ensure your learning solutions' effectiveness by monitoring their impact.

Here's an example: During a staff meeting, you're informed by the management team that "the last training initiative did not work" to increase sales revenue. What should you do? The answer depends on what the system requires in that situation:

> Did the training fail because the selected vendor didn't deliver as promised? You may want to evaluate other vendors and other solutions to deliver the value required—after clearly defining what "failure" means—and how it can be measured more effectively.

> Did the training fail because it had no visible metrics defined to show results beyond overall revenue? You may want to define other indicators of success (behavior change, increased knowledge, shorter sales cycles) to measure and evaluate.

> Did the training fail because there was no on-the-job reinforcement? You may want to help the sales leader see the need for such a solution through more proof points defined through the measurement process.

Throughout the *evaluate* phase, leadership commitment will be very important. Having the buy-in of the leadership team will help you establish a culture of training for results and continuous improvement.

The key actions of the *evaluate* phase are

> measuring the reactions of learners to the training
> measuring the level of learning that actually occurred during the training
> assessing how well the lessons being taught are transferred into actual behavior and habits over time
> assessing and doing your best to measure the impact training has on performance results
> using what is learned in the evaluation process to improve sales-wide learning plans and personal development plans.

The key outcomes of the *evaluate* phase are

> knowing how sales training initiatives are being received and what impact they are having on performance

▶ gaining insights about how to continuously improve your professional sales development programs

▶ gathering information that can be used to measure the return on the time and money invested in professional development

▶ understanding the four levels of evaluation and how to integrate them into your sales training initiatives.

Chapter 8 covers the *evaluate* phase in greater detail.

■ ■ ■

Chapters 4–8 work together to help you

▶ gather information about business goals, the current state of business results, the current state of the sales team, known best practices, and the resources available

▶ conduct gap analyses to help identify problem areas to be addressed and to better target sales training and development solutions for them

▶ assess your options for building or buying content, using SMEs, and developing reusable content

▶ make decisions about which training methods to use to best support the learning process.

 Getting It Done

This chapter helped you understand how to design sales training with impact. It focused on understanding the foundation of instructional design, while helping you create and revise training programs with speed and efficiency. To help you apply what you have learned, let's take a look at a traditional seven-step sales process (or sales methodology). The process used here follows the chronological steps that occur as a seller interacts with a buyer. To design sales training with impact, you want to focus on enabling salespeople to sell. Your sales training programs should identify the best practices available to your team. When you're done analyzing your sales process, you'll have the ability to customize your sales training approach to help your sales team sell with greater agility and flexibility. Each section below explains one of the seven steps, offers suggestions for elements to include in your training design, cautions about potential challenges, and suggests typical content you'll need to understand to design your sales training solutions effectively.

Step 1: Prospecting—This relates to the company or sales rep's ability to identify and connect with potential customers. In some organizations, the company invests money in advertising and turns these prospected leads over to the rep. Many firms expect the salesperson to find these prospects and initiate a sales dialogue.

> ▶ *Suggested design elements*—brainstorming with other sales team members; lecture on organizations; meetings and trade shows where prospects gather.
> ▶ *What to look out for*—sales team members should be taught to be very sensitive to the time invested in finding a prospect. Joining associations and attending trade shows should be scrutinized, even quantified, to determine their value as resources to land new business.
> ▶ *Typical content*—lists of resources where ideal buyers tend to gather.

Step 2: Pre-approach—This is the homework or research step of the selling process. It is essential and easy today for a salesperson to gather data on a company and even details on the specific prospect. Preparing this information prior to initiating a conversation arms a salesperson with details that help paint a broad picture about the company, its roles in its industry, and more. This effort positions the rep as a sales pro who understands as much as possible about the environment he or she will encounter when selling to this firm.

> ▶ *Suggested design elements*—lecture, demonstration of web and company resources for researching.
> ▶ *What to look out for*—sales team members should have some specific resources where they can quickly gather data, then take the time to study it before engaging a prospect. This should not take much time and, ideally, should be done where they have access to buyers outside selling hours.
> ▶ *Typical content*—databases and reference sources, either online or in print form.

Step 3: Qualifying—Qualifying involves sorting through leads to determine which are worthy of the sales rep's time and attention. Chasing poor prospects is a serious problem with most sales organizations, and a sales team member needs to be realistic in his or her investment of time with potential customers. This qualification process can occur prior to engaging prospects (through print or online methods), or it can be used in initial conversations between sales team members and prospects, to identify whether to pursue the relationship.

▶ *Suggested design elements*—brainstorm and/or model elevator speeches; role play opening dialogues with prospects; group discussion; question-and-answer exercises to identify great prospects versus poor ones; video or live simulation of good and bad prospects so sales team members can distinguish the difference.

▶ *What to look out for*—the company should help a salesperson identify exact criteria that make for a great prospect. The salesperson then should learn to turn his or her back on those prospects who don't fit. Simply put, the best sales team members spend more time with the best prospects.

▶ *Typical content*—analysis of existing best customers to determine what a best prospect is; list of qualifying questions based on those criteria.

Step 4: Presenting—The presentation is an opportunity for the salesperson to begin deepening the relationship by attempting to match his or her company's offerings to the needs of the prospect. This is also when training needs to focus on helping a salesperson develop outstanding questioning skills. This step of the process is defined by a commitment of both parties to discuss and determine whether further steps will be taken to discover whether the selling company can best serve the buying company. This is also when most sales team members begin to encounter resistance in the process.

▶ *Suggested design element*—video or live demonstration of a pitch; brainstorming and group discussion to craft the best language to present the company and its offerings; role play to simulate buyer/seller encounters; ride-alongs with sales team members to observe successful behavior.

▶ *What to look out for*—this is the most complex and lengthiest portion of the sales process. Sales team members should quickly get to the point by asking questions to determine how to best present to the prospect in front of them (or on the phone). In essence, a salesperson must be able to adapt and change direction in a conversation to match the buyer's interests, while advancing the sale toward the close. Setting boundaries on the time allowed for the presentation helps a salesperson maintain focus and respects the buyer's time.

▶ *Typical content*—bullet-point list of highlights for this conversation, including company history, best customers, benefits offered, and problems solved; list of potent questions to determine how serious the prospect is about buying the rep's solutions; possible coaching on speaking and presentation skills.

Step 5: Overcoming objections—This is where the selling process can get quite intense for sales team members. Prospects challenge solutions, pricing, delivery options, and more. A sales rep's ability to handle resistance is often one of the truest measures of her or his ability to succeed in a sales role. Typically, a company might encounter five or six basic objections to its offerings. Enabling sales team members to handle those basic objections expertly and smoothly is key to training success, particularly with new sales team members.

▶ *Suggested design elements*—demonstration and role play; brainstorming responses to objections; question-and-answer sessions, with experienced sales team members leading the discussions; documentation on objection responses for sales team members to keep handy; ride-alongs with sales reps to observe successful behavior.

▶ *What to look out for*—Focusing on those top five or six objections is the key to success in this step. Individual sales team members should be able to think of three or more responses to each objection. During role play, these responses should be practiced in a relaxed, confident, and professional manner. Be careful with sales team members who get anxious or defensive when they meet resistance, because that type of behavior will erode goodwill and eliminate any progress made prior to that point in the sales process.

▶ *Typical content*—comprehensive list of problems and top objections presented by buyers, matched with multiple responses to each; focused and dedicated role play to get sales team members comfortable in dealing with resistant prospects.

Step 6: Closing—Closing is to selling what a first-place finish is to racing. The key to closing effectively is based on the sales team member's ability to move the conversation toward completion and to know when to ask the buyer to buy. Closing questions are phrases that test the buyer's belief about working with the seller's offerings. The language choices might vary from one rep to another. The time to ask might vary from buyer to buyer. But if the purpose of the selling relationship is to end it with a "yes" (a purchase) or a "no" (disqualified prospect), then the closing gives sellers their true focus on the job.

- ▶ *Suggested design elements*—demonstration and role play; group discussion to create lists of closing questions; ride-alongs with sales team members to observe successful behavior.
- ▶ *What to look out for*—be cautious of sales team members who are great at conversing, but don't have the strength to ask the buyer to buy. Focus is the key here. You want salespeople to know when they are near the end of a conversation that the prospect will buy, or say goodbye, or set another meeting. Potent closing language, probably shared by others in the training environment, can be very helpful for rookies or weaker-performing sales team members.
- ▶ *Typical content*—closing questions; exercises that develop ability to set next steps when the buyer doesn't buy.

Step 7: Following-up—Closing isn't the end of the game. Follow-up is the last step. It involves fulfillment of the promises made by the selling company. Here is where the new customer is going to be delighted or disappointed by his or her decision. Follow-up done well is essential to eliminating buyers' remorse. Staying connected to customers also serves another purpose: It helps a salesperson get good-quality and well-qualified referrals. Doing so eliminates some of the earlier steps in the sales process. It's good to remember that the sale is not complete when the buyer signs an agreement. It's truly complete after the check clears the bank or after the guarantee period is over. Deep customer relationships are profoundly satisfying to a salesperson who often encounters a great deal of rejection in the course of her or his selling life.

- ▶ *Suggested design elements*—lecture on steps to complete the sale, including introduction of support personnel; demonstration on forms and processes used to complete fulfillment; brainstorming and group discussion on requesting referrals after the sale is complete.
- ▶ *What to look out for*—this last step is about implementing a fulfillment process that gives the buyer what he or she bought. The company should determine exactly what that is, prior to the sale's completion. Don't forget to build into this step the request for referrals from the new client!
- ▶ *Typical content*—introduction to support personnel and procedures; coaching on language for requesting referrals.

Phase 1: Exploring the Sales Environment

Brian W. Lambert

- -

What's Inside This Chapter

In this chapter, you'll learn

▶ How to explore the sales environment

▶ How to describe your sales team culture

▶ How to define existing performance gaps within any sales culture

▶ How to quantify business goals

▶ How your sales team is organized

▶ The five-whys approach to exploration

▶ 10 tools for exploration.

From the roles you have to play, the way meetings are run, and the way you have to manage your internal organization, sales culture is important. Obviously, you can't change sales culture by yourself, but as a sales trainer, you play a crucial role.

More important, you can't tie learning solutions to specific needs without a thorough understanding of the sales culture that exists within the departments, regions, or territories you serve. There can be more than one type of sales culture at play, and you'll have to work within them all.

Many sales trainers have been short-lived in the profession because they didn't understand how much the sales culture within an organization could affect their jobs and roles. It can be extremely frustrating at times when you find that your biggest barrier to success is your own organization—and the possible lack of support that you need to succeed fully.

Just like a map that points out the "you are here" spot to help you begin navigating your path to a desired destination, this section will serve as your road map to identifying, understanding, and navigating through five types of sales culture. What does it take to demonstrate and ratchet up sales success? Many believe it's as simple as this motto: "More activity leads to more success." But the most successful sales professionals realize that their success ultimately depends on their ability to drive results, and that includes *everything*—driving cost reductions in the sales organization, becoming more efficient in the sales position, and ensuring profitability in the buyer/seller relationship, to name only a few.

Types of Sales Culture

Figure 4-1 illustrates the five sales cultures that may exist in an organization: (1) individual sales performance, (2) defined sales outcomes, (3) measurement and evaluation, (4) recognized business value, and (5) sustained revenue growth. This section will take a detailed look at each of the cultures. If you'd like to make a quick assessment of the dominant sales culture in your organization, see the "Getting It Done" section at the end of this chapter. The ensuing discussion will help you see how the culture that dominates in your workplace may or may not support your efforts to design, develop, and deliver successful sales training.

Noted

Exploration is really the essence of the human spirit.
—Frank Borman, NASA astronaut and engineer

Figure 4-1. Types of Sales Cultures

Sustained Revenue Growth	←	Conduct regular gap analyses and make improvements
Recognized Business Value	←	Improve information flow with technology
Measurement and Evaluation	←	Align non-sales processes and metrics with the sales process
Defined Sales Outcomes	←	Standardize the sales process and sales metrics
Individual Sales Performance	←	Define the sales process against "How your customers buy"

Culture of Individual Sales Performance

Shown at the bottom left-hand side of the graphic in figure 4-1, the culture of individual sales performance represents the worst-case scenario in alignment with and support for your work. Within this culture, salespeople must operate as "lone wolves" able to rise above the inefficiencies of their organization. But this doesn't represent a world-class sales organization. This culture is characterized by a lack of organizationwide focus on what it takes to sell professionally. As a result, on the sales team it's every person for himself or herself. Communication is limited and political savvy is a key element of success. This type of culture creates salespeople who feel they must achieve success on their own. They also feel they need to manage the often-misaligned jobs and responsibilities of colleagues who are internally focused instead of market focused. These salespeople are constantly confounded by misaligned processes that seem to conflict with sales activity. As a result, the organization appears shortsighted and reactionary; and no foundation is created on which to build trust and develop lasting value for customers.

A typical but not all-inclusive list of outputs routinely witnessed within this type of sales culture could be the following:

▶ Pre-purchase expectations are set by sales professionals but not delivered by the organization.

▶ Marketing collateral doesn't align with the sales message.

▶ The salesperson has to retrieve information within the selling organization, often with little support.

▶ The sales professional must correct and manipulate organizational messages to make them more relevant.

Key actions required for success within this type of selling culture are focusing your sales training efforts on defining the existing sales process against how your buyers buy and making sure your learning and development solutions facilitate, rather than hinder, the sales process.

Culture of Defined Sales Outcomes

The culture of defined sales outcomes represents organizational alignment and support at its most basic level (figure 4-1). I'm hopeful that your organization is at least at this level. Here, the selling organization has instituted many key performance improvements that you can leverage to develop your training solutions. It's also at this level where the organization has established remediation strategies to address internal miscommunication issues; redefine roles and responsibilities; and reset expectations with marketing, sales, customer service, and fulfillment professionals. The organization also may have established a relationship management structure to create winning relationships, as well as procedures to quantify customer service, sales, and marketing outcomes. Metrics may now exist to help track process outcomes, and mechanisms are in place to detect and address revenue target deviations. And the organization may have established engagement management processes to request new services as needed, and may have developed benchmarking strategies to continually assess salesforce competitiveness.

A typical (but not all-inclusive) list of outputs routinely witnessed within this type of culture could be as follows:

▶ Focused sales techniques are used by most sales professionals.

▶ Positive, work-related relationships exist between sales colleagues.

▶ Rapport and trust exist among sales organization members.

▶ Documentation is prepared and delivered in a manner that requires little revision by the sales professional.

▶ Processes and their impact on products or services are assessed.

▶ Timelines are mostly kept, and correspondence is generally accurate.

▶ There are psychological factors surrounding the buying/selling relationship.

Key actions required for success within this type of selling culture are standardizing the sales process and sales metrics across your organization through sales training and coaching, and developing sales tools that the team can use to facilitate formal and informal learning.

Culture of Measurement and Evaluation

The culture of measurement (figure 4-1) takes a more proactive approach. The organization has set revenue targets that are reported regularly, and it uses change management processes within a solution-focused selling environment. Escalation management processes are established to address customer service issues, and business continuity processes are implemented to ensure superb support of the sales and marketing function to drive revenue. The sales function has standards that are benchmarked against other organizations at least once a year, and business and information technology measures are correlated and reported regularly, as they pertain to sales efforts.

A typical (but not all-inclusive) list of outputs routinely witnessed within this type of culture might be as follows:

▶ The desired impact on the business is achieved.

▶ Goods or services are delivered as customers expect.

▶ Return-on-investment numbers are met.

▶ Measurements of success are achieved.

▶ Project is within scope (if applicable).

The key action required for success within this type of selling culture is aligning nonsales processes and metrics with your sales process through multiple levels (and types) of training, so that each level of individual and organization need can be addressed through formal and informal training and coaching strategies.

Culture of Recognized Business Value

The culture of recognized business value (figure 4-1) represents a dedicated and sustained effort to achieve world-class sales excellence. The organization has developed professional standards that align with industry standards, and it leverages success stories. The organization is effective in driving costs out of the sales organization, while it improves business processes and increases buyer responsiveness. Sales teams meet forecasts and are supported by management processes that have established sales plans. The organization can alert the correct departments and business units when there are competitive threats, and sales processes are integrated and mostly automated. The organization has defined and ingrained sales processes that are based on best practices or their equivalents. Single points of weakness are quickly and adequately addressed. There is a supportive compensation plan in force, and the marketing organization drives market expansion and awareness.

A typical (but not all-inclusive) list of outputs routinely witnessed within this type of culture might be as follows:

▶ Most buyers make renewal or rebuy decisions.
▶ It is easy to up-sell or cross-sell more products or services.
▶ Buyers are willing to explore the impact the selling organization may have on their organizations.
▶ Creating strategic partnerships is easy.
▶ Trust, rapport, and communication flow are prevalent.

The key action required for success within this type of selling culture is improving sales team processes and effectiveness and the flow of information by incorporating technology in the training and development approach.

Culture of Sustained Revenue Growth

The culture of sustained revenue growth (shown at the pinnacle of the graphic in figure 4-1) represents a fully capable and aligned sales organization. Repeatable and definable selling processes exist throughout the organization. Supportive processes (for example, marketing, sales, and customer service initiatives and efforts) align with the sales function and are managed in a systematic and holistic way. Quantified measures of sales efforts exist. All managers understand what the sales professional needs, how other departments can support the sales professional, and how their role as internal stakeholders contributes equally to an ability to create revenue performance. Learning and best practices exist and are institutionalized. A solid understanding of organizational vision, mission, and goals is thoroughly ingrained through a common language and proper alignment with the customer.

A typical (but not all-inclusive) list of outputs routinely witnessed within this type of culture might be as follows:

- ▶ All sales goals are accomplished.
- ▶ There is proper alignment within the sales organization.
- ▶ There is no role ambiguity between sales and marketing functions.
- ▶ Sales targets are continuously exceeded.
- ▶ A selling cycle management maturity model is leveraged and enhanced with feedback mechanisms adopted.
- ▶ At least 70 percent of new proposals are won.
- ▶ Technology is leveraged to enable strategic business initiatives.
- ▶ Training for sales professionals provides continual improvement opportunities.

Key actions required for success within this type of selling culture are conducting regular gap analyses and making constant improvements.

■ ■ ■

In summary, sales professionals not only have accountability and responsibility for driving revenue, but within the buyer/seller relationship, they also play many roles in which they're expected to excel. Your job as a sales trainer is to understand the sales culture(s) that exist within your sales organization so that sales professionals can maximize their time investment, effectively run productive meetings, and skillfully maneuver within the organization's sales culture.

Defining Existing Performance Gaps Within Any Sales Culture

Gap analysis is the process used to determine where you are and where you want to be. In other words, this is when you reveal the desired state of performance and compare it with the current state of performance. The discrepancy between how your sales organization wishes to perform and how it actually performs is known as a "performance gap." When you conduct a gap analysis, you gather information on your sales team's operational results—both the *desired* operational results and the *current* operational results. In addition to learning about the business's operational results, you also have to explore salesperson performance as it relates to achieving the defined operational results. In other words, you want to know what salesperson actions or behaviors will lead to these operational results. Salesperson performance is the foundation on which operational results rest—and that's where you come in. If employee performance doesn't at least meet a set of minimum standards, the business can't meet its goals. On the other hand, if employee performance meets or exceeds expectations, the business will meet or exceed its goals. Just as you must discover the desired and current states of the business's operational results, you must discover the desired and current employee performances.

In this first phase of the Rapid Development Blueprint, you must conduct a proper performance gap analysis to quantify the current state of whatever is being measured, quantify the desired state, and discover the size and source of any "gap" that exists between the two. A good performance gap analysis consists of

▶ quantifying gaps between desired and actual sales results
▶ identifying competency gaps that may be contributing to the results gap
▶ breaking larger competency gaps into manageable, incremental steps
▶ translating competency gaps into specific learning elements.

To define the performance gap, you must know what specifically the organization will achieve differently as a result of your sales training and development solution. More important, you must understand what the end learning experience will be for your sales team. Below are some questions you must answer to do this effectively:

1. What are the current business results, stated in measurable terms?
2. What would the business results look like if performance were where it should be?
3. What internal factors support or prevent the desired state?
4. What external factors support or prevent the desired state?

When you're clear on the performance gap, you can define what specific skills and knowledge the learners will need to have at the end of the learning session to address this gap.

Many sales trainers I know believe that the requests from training they receive from sales managers are often related to a request for content, rather than a request for a specific performance outcome. That's why it's important that you ask the necessary questions to clearly identify the desired outcomes. Only after you have defined the outcomes should you move on to identify the content that should be included. (See the next chapter for a discussion of the *examine* phase.)

Quantifying Business Goals

According to Dana Gaines Robinson and James C. Robinson, authors of *Performance Consulting: A Practical Guide for HR and Learning Professionals* (2008),

> Business goals are the measures organizations use to track their progress toward achieving their business needs and goals. Business goals are usually expressed in hard numbers and can include measures such as

> ▶ percentages
> ▶ customer satisfaction index
> ▶ response time
> ▶ sales per salesperson.

A business goal can be communicated in terms of performance gaps or competency gaps. The gap is simply the difference between the current and the desired performances or competencies. It is clearer to understand if the gap is stated in terms of numerical data, but can also be stated in terms of trends.

Some of the questions you must be prepared to address include these:

1. What is the scope of the business problem to be solved, or the information that needs to be disseminated?
2. How does the gap map against corporate vision, mission, and current business priorities?
3. What alternatives does the business have for addressing this training need?

   ▶ What is the projected cost of each alternative?
   ▶ How long will each alternative take to deploy?
   ▶ What type of time footprint will each alternative make on the productive selling time of the participants?
   ▶ What is the projected effectiveness of each alternative?

> ### Think About This
>
> Selling is not simply about encouraging someone to buy a product or service; it's also about listening, analyzing, problem solving, and persuading. Selling is about valuable conversations and relevant communications designed to help the salesperson move the sales process forward by becoming a trusted adviser. As a sales trainer, you're in a position to positively influence these dynamics!

4. How much of an impact can having this knowledge or developing these new skills have on sales performance?
5. How much is it costing the business each week/month/quarter/year to *not* address this issue?
6. How much of an impact can this training program have on customer acquisition, experience, and loyalty?
7. How can this initiative affect employee satisfaction, morale, and loyalty?
8. Assuming that you train for results, what type of potential return can the business expect from this investment?

Tool 4-1 is a checklist you can use to guide you in selecting sources to contact for information about business goals and about gaps that may exist between desired and current performances and competencies. The sources are categorized according to specific potential business situations.

Understanding How the Sales Team Is Organized

A sales territory is the geography assigned to a specific salesperson where he or she can find prospects and convert them to wildly happy, long-term clients. To sell a product or service, an organization has to decide on the segmentation strategy needed as part of its go-to-market sales approach. "Segmentation" is the slicing and dicing of a market to form territories.

When the market is segmented, the organization will be able to determine the best strategy to cover the resulting territories, such as a mix of direct or indirect sales strategies. There are four ways that the sales leadership team may segment a market to define territories:

Tool 4-1. Checklist of Potential Sources for Information on Business Goals

Situation description	Sources
New technology: introduction of new technology to the organization may require changes in individual performance.	• Executives • Information technology department • Marketing department • Performers • Subject matter experts
New employees or expanding employee roles: the organization hires new employees or wants to prepare employees for additional new responsibilities.	• Executives • Human resources department • Line management • Recently hired performers
Business opportunity: introduction of something new to the organization may require changes in individual performance: • new product • new business philosophy or strategy.	• Executives • Marketing department • Performers
Business problem: the organization needs to respond to a problem in which business goals are not being met, apparently because of a problem in individual or group performance.	• Customers • Employees • Executives • Managers • Performers • Subject matter experts

1. **Geographic segmentation** is a straightforward approach that defines a territory based on

    ▶ country (such as the entire United States)
    ▶ region (such as the Northeast or Southwest)
    ▶ state (or mixture of states)
    ▶ city (or major metropolitan area).

Editor's Notebook

One of my sales training colleagues met with me to discuss a new sales training program she was designing. She immediately began talking about the number of days the class would last, the types of activities she was going to use in the class, and the way in which she had updated the evaluation forms to capture new and improved data regarding the course. She was excited about the changes she'd made on the branding of the slides and participant materials, and about the amount of information in each. More important, she was very happy with the way her team worked together to develop the course on time and within budget. After she gave me all the details, she paused and asked what I thought of the new course. I simply asked, "What business need does this course fill, and how will you know if it worked or not?" She didn't have an answer. In fact, she was upset that I'd asked the question in the first place. It wasn't what she expected. Through the next few weeks, we worked to analyze the new course within the context of the business challenges we identified together; we also made some crucial changes to bring the course into alignment, while reinforcing some key messages from the leadership team. The course was well received and is still in use today.

2. **Account segmentation** is accomplished by assigning an account to a specific person or team. This can be done by using the size of the account (total revenue from the account) or on a first-come/first-served basis.

3. **Vertical market segmentation** groups all accounts within one area of specialty by the types of customers, including

   ▶ business-to-business—businesses that sell to other businesses

   ▶ business-to-consumer—businesses that sell to consumers

   ▶ business-to-government—businesses that sell to the federal, state, or local government

   ▶ business-to-association—businesses that sell to nonprofit and for-profit trade or charity associations.

4. **Channel segmentation** uses a distribution channel (companies that resell a product) to reach customers. Channel marketing consists of developing go-to-market plans, educating channel marketers, and motivating the members of the marketing channel to promote products and services. An example of this would be a company that sells Hewlett-Packard software and hardware bundled within its solution.

Types of Sales Positions

Professional selling occurs through several types of communication and interaction strategies. Each of these sales strategies has unique aspects that make it relevant for particular selling situations.

Think About This

Did you know that the word "sell" is derived from the Icelandic word *selja* and the Anglo-Saxon word *syllan*—both of which mean "to serve" or "to give"?

As depicted in figure 4-2, there are two primary groupings of selling strategies—direct channels and indirect channels. A channel is how the company decides to go to market and sell its products or services. Every organization must make a choice on how to sell—that is, either directly to the end user (usually with some point-of-sale enabler, such as a salesperson) or indirectly through a reseller, partner, or alliance.

Figure 4-2. Direct and Indirect Selling Channels

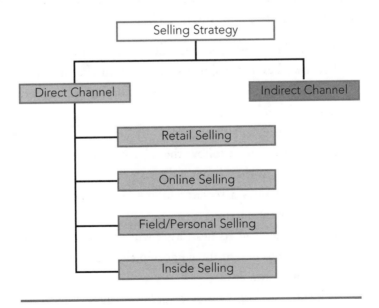

Indirect sales channels as part of professional selling are big business. Indirect sales organizations don't deliver a product or service to an actual end user. For example, Hewlett-Packard's primary business is selling computers and printers. To provide a complete solution to customers, they may offer consulting services via subcontractors—that is, through an indirect sales channel.

The other channel in figure 4-2 represents direct sales. In direct sales, there are four primary selling strategies that organizations may use to sell products or services directly to the end user: retail sales, online sales, field or personal sales, and inside sales.

By understanding how the sales team is organized, you'll gain a more thorough understanding of the context and environment that you must operate within. With this context, you'll be able to complete a more robust exploration.

The Five-Whys Approach to Exploration

The best exploration tool I have found is the "Five Whys" adapted from the Six Sigma discipline. To use this approach, you pose the identified performance gap as a question and then ask "Why?" up to five more times regarding each iterative answer. By the fifth *why,* you'll find the root problem or cause of the issue. For example, if the performance gap statement is "In the first quarter, sales were 10 percent below our goals for this region," the five *whys* might go like this:

Question 1. Why didn't sales associates reach their sales targets?

Answer 1. Because they often got distracted from the sales process by the large volume of communication, information, and processes they have to know and follow.

Question 2. Why did they get distracted?

Answer 2. Because they don't follow the sales process step by step, and that contributes to their level of distraction.

Question 3. Why don't sales associates follow every step of the sales model with every interaction?

Answer 3. Because they sometimes forget what the steps are. Or they don't know how to determine what step they're in with each individual client or customer.

Question 4. Why do they forget the steps or have trouble identifying what step they're in?

Answer 4.   Because they don't have the sales process memorized.

Question 5.   Why don't they have the sales process memorized?

Answer 5.   Because the sales organization doesn't provide any tools to help them memorize it, and the technology isn't customized to map to the sales process in place.

From here, you could explore alternative solutions to the performance issue with the sales team.

10 Issues and 10 Tools for Exploration

Whether you have two months or two hours within which to complete your exploration process, you must address 10 key issues during the *explore* phase of the blueprint. These are the issues and the questions you should ask in your exploration:

1. **Executive sponsorship**—Who "owns" the future training initiative within the organization? Remember, there may be multiple owners.
2. **Goals for the initiative**—What are the business and emotional goals by which this initiative will be measured?
3. **Perceived problem**—What is the problem that leadership believes needs to be addressed?
4. **Underlying issues**—What are the potential root sources for the problem?
5. **Size and scope of the problem**—How pervasive is this problem, and how much is it costing the business not to address it?
6. **Time and budget for the solution**—What is the lead time available to prepare a solution? How much time is allowed for training? What is the budget available for the initiative?
7. **Current state of the sales team(s)**—What is the profile of the prospective audience (that is, participants' education and experience; demographic makeup; perceptions of the problem; business climate within which they operate)? What is the impact the perceived problem may be having on the audience's performance and earning potential?
8. **Competencies to be addressed**—What are the identified best practices (knowledge, skills, and abilities) to be incorporated in the training solution?
9. **Logistics**—How many people will be involved? Where are they located? What are the available technologies? When are upcoming events? Are

there culture and language issues? Are there other factors that might affect delivery?

10. **Existing solutions**—How has the firm addressed this issue in the past? What resources are available from training solutions that have been employed previously?

There is a broad range of tools you can use to help facilitate the exploration process. Here are 10 tools that may be available to you:

1. **ASTD World-Class Sales Competency Model**—The model can be used as a benchmark to define and develop best practices to deploy across the sales organization and as a diagnostic tool to identify gaps in the knowledge, skills, and abilities of a sales organization.

2. **Self-assessment inventory**—This enables individuals to give input to the professional development process by assessing their own strengths and weaknesses and helping prioritize training and development needs.

3. **Peer/leader assessment inventory**—This tool enables peers and leaders to provide an assessment of team members. When combined with a self-assessment, this third-party input lends additional context and perspective to identifying training needs.

4. **Assessment results summaries**—A summary tool brings together the results of both self-assessment and peer/leader assessments to present a clearer picture of sales training and development needs and priorities.

5. **Commercial profiling tools**—There is a broad array of commercially available profiling tools designed to assess and document such traits as personality, communications style, values, and skills.

6. **Survey forms**—Survey guides tailored to your business and the sales teams you support lead you through an orderly exploration process.

7. **Corporate documents**—Current copies of these important corporate documents are especially helpful: organization charts, job descriptions, annual reports, compensation plans, mission statements and shared values, marketing materials, sales reports, and procedures manuals.

8. **Technology testing**—Internally developed or commercially available tools can test an individual's competency level with the technology tools she or he must use on the job.

9. **Sales team analysis tools**—Sales executives and sales team leaders use these to take a more strategic look at their sales organization and the issues that may need to be addressed to support the achievement of strategic objectives.

10. **Sales training diagnostic tools**—These tools assess the value and effectiveness of existing training materials.

■ ■ ■

This chapter has given you a firm foundation for understanding the sales culture and environment within which you operate. Although often overlooked, this *explore* phase is a key determinant of your success because it ties the remaining phases of the Rapid Development Blueprint to a solid understanding of trends, goals, and desired outcomes at the organization level. Now that you have completed your exploration process, you can move into the next phase of the blueprint—the *examine* phase.

Getting It Done

Think of your current sales organization, or a sales organization you've worked for in the past. Use the following assessment questions to identify the type of sales culture(s) that dominates in that sales organization.

Instructions: Circle "Yes" or "No" after each statement to indicate if the statement is descriptive of your sales organization. Tally the number of "Yes" answers in each culture area. If you have three or more "Yes" responses in any culture area, that culture is a part of your sales organization. You may have two or more types of culture represented in the sales organization, but one tends to be dominant over the others.

Culture of Individual Sales Performance

Key action required for success within this type of culture: Define your sales process against how buyers buy

1. Pre-purchase expectations are set by sales professionals, but not delivered by the organization.   Yes   No
2. Marketing collateral doesn't align with the sales message.   Yes   No

3. The salesperson has to retrieve information within the
    selling organization, often with little support.   Yes   No
4. The sales professional must correct and manipulate
    organizational messages to become more relevant.   Yes   No

Culture of Defined Sales Outcomes

Key action required for success within this type of culture: standardize the sales process
and the sales metrics

1. Focused sales techniques are used by most sales professionals.   Yes   No
2. Positive, work-related relationships exist between sales
    colleagues.   Yes   No
3. Rapport and trust exist among sales organization members.   Yes   No
4. Documentation is prepared and delivered in a manner
    that requires little reworking by the sales professional.   Yes   No
5. Processes and their impact on products or services are assessed. Yes   No
6. Timelines are mostly kept, and most correspondence is accurate.   Yes   No
7. Psychological factors surround the buying/selling relationship.   Yes   No

Culture of Measurement

Key action required for success within this type of culture: align nonsales processes and
metrics with your sales process

1. The desired impact on the business is achieved.   Yes   No
2. Goods or services are delivered as customers expect.   Yes   No
3. Return-on-investment numbers are met.   Yes   No
4. Measurements of success are achieved.   Yes   No
5. Project is within scope (if applicable).   Yes   No

Culture of Recognized Business Value

Key action required for success within this type of selling culture: improve effectiveness
and information flow with technology

1. Most buyers make renewal or rebuy decisions.   Yes   No
2. Up-selling or cross-selling of products or services is easy.   Yes   No
3. Buyers are willing to explore the impact the selling
    organization may have on their organizations.   Yes   No

4. Creation of strategic partnerships is easy.   Yes   No
5. Trust, rapport, and communication flow are prevalent.   Yes   No

Culture of Sustained Revenue Growth

Key action required for success within this type of selling culture: conduct regular gap analyses and make continual improvements

1. All sales goals are accomplished.   Yes   No
2. There is proper alignment within the sales organization.   Yes   No
3. There is no role ambiguity between sales and
    marketing functions.   Yes   No
4. Sales targets are continuously exceeded.   Yes   No
5. A selling cycle management maturity model is leveraged and
    enhanced with feedback mechanisms adopted.   Yes   No
6. At least 70 percent of new proposals are won.   Yes   No
7. Technology is leveraged to enable strategic business initiatives.   Yes   No
8. Training for sales professionals is provided for continuous
    improvement opportunities.   Yes   No

5

Phase 2: Examining Sales Team Goals and Needs

Paul Smith

What's Inside This Chapter

In this chapter, you'll learn

► How to respond to training requests
► How to conduct a needs assessment
► How to determine who needs to attend training
► Alternatives to classroom training
► How to target the right participants
► Methods for gathering data
► How to use a training contract.

This chapter focuses on the second phase of the Rapid Development Blueprint for Sales Training, discussed in chapter 3. The *examine* phase is extremely important to your success as a sales trainer because you will be able to tie the broader sales environment you explored in the previous phase to needs that are specific to your sales team. Great sales trainers are like doctors who make an appropriate medical diagnosis before they prescribe a recommended course of action. They diagnose before they prescribe.

To effectively diagnose sales training needs before recommending a sales training solution, you have to conduct a proper needs analysis. Conducting a needs analysis within your sales organization ensures that you have the right participants in your classes, deliver the appropriate materials at the right time, and ensure learning transfer takes place each and every time.

In this chapter, we'll explore the many facets of conducting a proper analysis, we'll explore the uniqueness of the sales training environment in relation to that analysis, and you'll learn to leverage a sound approach to determining audience needs.

Responding to Training Requests the Right Way

Let's face it, most trainers find it hard to say "no" to a training request. After all, requests come from sales managers who need us, and we don't want to let them down. But effectively serving our sales team sometimes means clarifying specific requests, or even saying "no." When your experience and research tell you that training is not the solution, or when the specific training requested isn't aligned with organization goals or is either too broad or too narrow to address the real business need, you've got to think like a salesperson and ask more probing questions, listen, and work diligently to co-create a solution that works from a learning perspective and a sales perspective. More important, you must have a plan.

Noted

All assessment is a perpetual work in progress.
—Linda Suskie, vice president of the Middle States Commission on Higher
Education

Here's a situation you may have experienced in your role as a trainer: The sales manager calls you, frustrated and a little panicked. She tells you her department just can't continue to operate the way it is now. She's got salespeople who aren't meeting their profitability and new business goals—and they aren't very good at overcoming buyer objections. She wants you to fix those problems and she asks you to conduct a training session next week—maybe teaching the sales reps some techniques for selling the company value.

OK, you're in an important role and one of the department members needs your help. Although "OK!" may seem like the proper response to a direct request, it actually could be overly reactive and ultimately may not serve your stakeholders—the sales rep learners and the customers they interact with daily.

Instead of telling the sales manager you'll get right on it, think like a salesperson and ask her some targeted probing questions—then listen to her responses:

▶ Has she identified a specific behavior that she feels is nonproductive and for which she is trying to identify the cause?

▶ Can the identified gap between current performance and desired performance truly be addressed through a training solution? Why or why not?

▶ Are there other underlying factors that contribute to the behavior in the sales team?

▶ When the training is rolled out, how will she know if it was successful or not? Will success actually be measured and documented over time?

▶ Who else needs to buy in to implement the final training solution? (Oftentimes, line managers are seen as roadblocks.)

▶ Do you or the sales manager need to document the current performance gap and then verify that the investment in training provides sufficient return?

Those questions that you ask should help influence your thinking. By asking them, you are beginning to conduct a sales training needs assessment in response to the training request.

Let's consider another example. A sales manager requests a training session on negotiation skills. Remember, your first task is to determine what the performance gap is. What does her team need to be able to negotiate better? Simply talking about "negotiating for a win–win situation" rarely produces the desired outcome of more results. (If it were that easy, everyone would be doing a lot more talking about it!) As a sales trainer, you have to dig deeper and find out why negotiation is an issue of concern. Is negotiation really the issue, or is it a symptom of a greater issue? You might ask yourself, the sales manager, and even the salespeople themselves questions such as these: What do people need to negotiate more effectively? What prevents this team from negotiating more win–win outcomes? Is there something else underneath the apparent issue of negotiation that is the real issue? In this example, you might determine that sales team members have poor communication skills in front of customers, especially when gaining final commitment. Poor communication is the source of the perceived lack of negotiation skills. When you've determined the issue, you can more easily define the performance gap. This is the performance gap in this example: "Salespeople need to more effectively communicate with their customers, especially at the time of final commitment." Based on that performance gap analysis, you can now begin to clearly define the learner outcomes. You may find an abundance of skills and knowledge that are associated with negotiation:

- ▶ listening skills
- ▶ questioning skills
- ▶ commitment-building skills
- ▶ product knowledge and industry knowledge
- ▶ business case/value articulation skills.

Based on your performance gap analysis, you've determined that communication is the core issue related to the perceived lack of negotiating ability. The question now becomes, What do you want the learners to be able to do at the end of this learning experience? The answer to that question forms the basis of your learner outcomes. Effective learner outcomes for this example might be stated in the following way: The learner will be able to

- ▶ understand the importance of communicating project status on every assignment
- ▶ effectively prioritize projects by asking three key questions on every assignment
- ▶ identify red-flag areas—potential challenges that might affect follow-through
- ▶ implement the project status update system.

In discovering all the relevant aspects of an identified problem and defining the needs of all the stakeholders involved in the problem and its solution, it's important to seek multiple perspectives. Merely getting one person's input or responding to one person's view of the problem is unlikely to create a successful solution that stands the test of time.

For example, although many sales managers focus on sales skills (questioning, negotiating, and closing skills), how robust is the product and industry training your organization delivers? On what tools and processes do you train to help your sales team stay productive? What about managers? Are they conducting great coaching conversations? Clearly, there's more to many sales challenges than the skills of just the salesperson. Your job is to help develop your sales team over time, with a continuous improvement approach. To do that, you may need to look at your organization from a systems perspective that focuses not only on the competencies required, but also on the way in which the competencies can be leveraged as a standard of excellence. What if you could help manage the talent (from recruitment to leadership development)? What if you could build learning plans that covered the needs of new onboarding sales team members as well as the needs of experienced members?

Taking a systems view and getting out of the "what class should we offer" mentality is important. And, depending on your sales organization, it's something you may be able to accomplish quickly or over a period of time. Just remember that having a consultative mindset can help you conduct the right needs analysis and lay the groundwork for long-lasting change.

Consider this scenario: A sales manager notices that a specific region consistently has lower sales numbers than comparable regions. He assumes the salespeople in that region don't have strong sales closing skills, so he asks the corporate sales trainer (we'll call her Jennifer) to develop a half-day workshop on "how to close effectively." Unfortunately, Jennifer doesn't have a consultative mindset, and she hasn't built a trusting partnership with the sales team. So, instead of asking questions, interviewing the target population, and performing a comprehensive needs analysis, she quickly designs and delivers the training requested. And it's a disaster. The sales team believes it was a complete waste of time. They lodge complaints against the sales manager for an ineffective training experience that provided no value, and Jennifer loses credibility in the eyes of the sales team. Certainly, the sales numbers aren't going to move—and that was the sales manager's original business goal.

What went wrong? Well, if Jennifer had made a few quick phone calls to salespeople in that region, she may have learned (1) the company management team has communicated that building relationships is the most important sales effort (more important than closing deals); and (2) the only metric that really matters is two face-to-face meetings per week booked in customer relationship management software by each salesperson, but the corporate virtual private network is often down so a salesperson's productivity appears to drop, intranet access is spotty, and it's hard to find the appropriate product knowledge when sales reps need it. Those factors are much more likely to be the cause of low sales numbers than are the sales reps' skills. You can deliver superb training all day, but it won't make an appreciable difference in adjusting the management team's approach, fixing technology, or facilitating product knowledge transfer.

If Jennifer delivered an ill-conceived training event to this population, it would not only waste time and money, it also might come with the following risks:

- **Insulted learners**—The salespeople in this region may already know how to sell; in fact, they may be really good at handling competitive threats and landing difficult sales. Making them sit through a sales course that contains material they already know will be demeaning and demoralizing.
- **Wasted resources**—Although there is a benefit to bringing the sales team together, the gathering's primary purpose is invalid. As such, it's a wasteful use of financial resources, human capital, and time.
- **Negative productivity in other regions**—In addition to any demoralizing impact that this training could have on the participants, the message sent to "more successful" regions may be interpreted to mean that those regions with lower performance are "rewarded" with more training and development time. Salespeople in those other regions may feel they don't need to continue putting so much effort into what they do if they feel they aren't provided similar access to such resources.
- **Missed opportunity**—If the sales manager had properly established the true reasons for the region's low numbers, Jennifer's training course could have incorporated information, tools, and resources to arm the salespeople to meet the unique challenges they face in the region.

For the reasons mentioned above, a needs analysis must involve more than just the department leader's opinion of what the team needs. Done correctly, a needs analysis will diminish the risks in any training initiative.

Starting Off on the Right Foot

In the ADDIE model of instructional design discussed in chapter 3, analysis is the first step. Many sales trainers will start with the needs analysis and skip the *explore* phase (chapter 4). But pause for a minute. I want you to think about why it's important to separate the needs analysis from your broader perspective on the sales profession and your sales organization. Why do you think it's better to have a deep understanding of the trends in selling, your sales team culture, and the broader challenge you face before you begin the needs analysis? Because this broader perspective from the *explore* phase of the Rapid Development Blueprint will help you develop an appropriate frame of mind for the needs analysis I discuss in this chapter. It is during this *examine* phase that the instructional "issue" is identified and validated. Just because training seems to be the obvious response to a situation doesn't mean that it truly is the most effective way to deal with the root problem at hand.

A key portion of the *examine* phase is conducting a needs analysis that involves more than a simple computer-based survey. It's crucial to incorporate as much human contact as possible in the needs analysis because it will yield much better results and will provide a much stronger foundation for the training you'll design and deliver in response. This is particularly true when you're dealing with salespeople because they want to be engaged as much as possible to feel they're playing an active part in focusing and creating the training.

It also is imperative to the success of the training that all stakeholders involved know exactly what training project parameters have been agreed to, what will or won't be included, and what content should be considered "out of scope." This type of group agreement establishes the project's goals up front and minimizes the opportunity for "scope creep"—the incremental enlargement of scope.

To help, here are some questions you'll need to address as you progress through this phase:

- Are there gaps between the employees' current skill levels and the skill levels required for the jobs?
- What will the learners need to understand to be engaged in improving their skills?
- What information or knowledge must the learners understand to improve?
- What do the learners need to be able to do better?
- What will the learners need to understand to assess their progress?

But the phase includes more than just gathering information about the gap that must be filled and the content that should be delivered. This phase also is where the target audience for the training will be identified and where you come to understand what participants already may or may not know about the subject matter.

> ## Think About This
>
> To validate your sales training, a needs assessment is critical in supporting the investment of sales training dollars.

Conducting a Needs Assessment

There are many resources on needs assessment available from ASTD. The resources include job aids, books, and conference content on the art and science of conducting a needs assessment.

No matter what methods you decide to use, the steps remain basically the same. You will

- identify the root problem
- develop a plan to resolve the issue
- gather data
- analyze the data
- make a final decision.

Identify the Root Problem

First, identify the root of the issue. This involves more than describing unsatisfying results; it goes straight to the underlying cause. This step makes it clear if training is truly the appropriate response and, if it is, it identifies the information your training will need to cover. For example, if your salespeople lack knowledge about a product or service they're selling, your course may focus on its features, benefits, and value as well as its functionality and appropriate uses. On the other hand, if salespeople struggle to stay motivated, your class may focus more on soft skills, such as goal setting, problem solving, and motivation.

A common issue that prompts sales training is the lack of individual salesperson performance. Although it's never good to isolate and single out an individual performer, your needs analysis can focus on aggregating individual problems. Lack of individual sales performance can happen for a lot of different reasons, such as

- poor time management
- lack of product knowledge

- underdeveloped technology skills
- inability to overcome objections
- selling beyond price
- lack of motivation or drive.

Never assume you know either the true cause of the problem or what the training needs are without first conducting your needs analysis. Start by asking these questions:

1. What knowledge and skills gaps seem to be contributing to a lack of performance?
2. Are these skills gaps at the novice or expert level (or both)?
3. What current solutions are managers putting in place to help overcome the challenges in performance?
4. Will a 180-degree tool (or 360-degree tool) help identify and prioritize specific needs? If so, what is the management stance on using such assessments?

When you understand the individual needs, you can begin to understand the aggregate needs in the sales team. Start by asking these questions:

1. Who is the target audience and what are their similarities and differences?
2. What are the current deficiencies to be addressed by this training?
3. What are the delivery options? Are there limitations of group size, location, or time?
4. What is the timeline for the stages of the training project (explore, examine, enable, execute, and evaluate)?
5. What is management's goal for results? How will they determine if the training has succeeded?

Develop a Plan for the Needs Assessment

The next step in conducting your needs assessment is to develop a plan to obtain information. Think like a project manager. Create a work plan that includes milestone dates to complete each task. The work plan template presented in tool 5-1 lists the tasks you need to complete, your timeline for doing so, and key stakeholders affected. Your work plan also should have a space to track progress and describe issues you discover. Remember that this template is just a shell. You'll add a great deal of detail for each task and activity needed to accomplish your needs assessment goals.

Tool 5-1. Work Plan for Assessing Training Needs

Task	Duration	Start	Finish	Stakeholders/ Key Contacts	Task Status
Initiate and design the research phase					
Perform gap analysis					
Define current state and desired outcome(s)					
Identify objectives for the needs assessment					
Gather Data					
Surveys					
Interviews					
Observations					
Focus groups					
Stakeholder consultations					
Analyze data to define problem and training goals					
Interpret data					
Identify training objective(s)					
Define recommendations and solutions					
Provide feedback to relevant stakeholders as needed					

Task	Duration	Start	Finish	Stakeholders/ Key Contacts	Task Status
Analyze audience needs, if training is needed					
Identify likely participants					
Consider alternative training methods/environments (for example, mentoring, coaching, e-learning, self-directed study)					
Describe impact of attendance on participants					
Develop action plan for training (track every detail and action necessary)					
Describe the best method and venue for training (for example, classroom training, mentoring, coaching, e-learning, self-directed study)					
Develop an evaluation plan that enables you to determine if the learning solution you implemented was successful					
Evaluate					
Design a means to assess knowledge transfer of participants					
Evaluate results					
Refine training as needed					

The work plan template helps you get an idea of optional approaches to gathering the data necessary to complete your assessment before moving forward. When using a work plan, you can focus clearly on the goals for your assessment.

The work plan tracks your progress along the way and acts as a working checklist of your challenges and accomplishments. It serves as a status report and helps you stay organized and focused. You may want to make your work plan available to stakeholders so they can track your progress as well.

Gather Data

Now it's time to gather your data! This means conducting a survey or focus group, making phone calls to members of the salesforce, and interviewing the sales team's manager. The key to gathering data is that you don't stop when you've identified one problem or issue. Keep using your resources. Continue your assessment until you feel confident you've gathered enough data to uncover all of your potential areas of opportunity for training. If your organization has a tolerance for using technology (such as 180- or 360-degree tools), use them to help build your case.

In addition to typical data-gathering approaches, sales trainers have other important data points to look at, such as these:

- **Sales numbers,** including cold calls, proposals, new sales, cross-sales and up-sales, and customer retention—Sales teams typically track these numbers, so they should be readily accessible. When you get access to the numbers, you can trend these same metrics yourself to become more proactive for your sales team. Even better, get a seat at the table during sales meetings to discuss them.
- **Lost sales**—These often can tell you as much as retained sales can. You even may reach out to those customers who've left, if doing so is within your company guidelines.
- **Customer demographics**—Believe it or not, looking at customer demographics can reveal potential problems or issues that you might not have considered. For example, could your salespeople have territories that are too large? If so, it's not a training issue. It's something that should be shared with (and handled by) leadership.
- **Recorded customer calls**—These are great sources of information about sales reps' weaknesses. They reveal where and what kind of sales training is needed, and they're a rich resource for coaching and feedback.

▶ **Accompanied calls**—When training has been requested for one or a small group of salespeople, go with them individually on sales calls and watch them in action. This is a great way to identify both helping and hindering behaviors.

Basic Rule

You should be "out and about" with your sales team on a regular basis. You should be seen as a regular in the field by the reps you help. They should consider you as one of their own, and as someone who "gets it." To do that, you need to be riding along with them, listening in on their customer calls, and asking probing questions to observe, motivate, and provide developmental feedback.

Here's an example of how using customer demographics and observing a salesperson in action can help you identify problems and potential solutions: John is a sales manager at an insurance company. He grew up in the Chicago suburbs, graduated from the University of Illinois three years ago, and has been working for your company ever since. He recently moved to a territory in rural Idaho—an area that's spread across a great number of miles. Unlike John, most of the other salespeople in that region grew up in farming communities. John is struggling with his sales numbers and is considerably off goal. As the trainer responsible for the territory, you have been asked by John's manager to ride along with John as he calls on clients to see if you can identify any performance issues. Watching John with his clients, you see that he's a very skilled salesperson. He explains the company products and services. He also understands his job and his role in relation to the overall corporate objectives. More important, he's friendly and very organized. However, after a day of riding with John, you're thinking that the problem may not be his ability to sell, but his inability to build rapport and relate to customers whose backgrounds and ways of thinking are different from his own. You ask John if it's OK to contact some of his customers. After making a few phone calls, you find that your instincts were right. In conducting this needs assessment, you've discovered that training isn't going to solve the problem—the issue is one of improper fit in job placement. At this point, you confidently can share your findings with John's manager and help in identifying alternative solutions for John's success.

Analyze Data

The fourth step in your needs assessment is to analyze the information you have in front of you. Consider the following questions:

1. Are outside influences making the sales goals unachievable?
2. Is there a lack of resources?
3. Have there been changes in the market?
4. Is something other than training causing the problem?
5. Do you have enough data to make an informed decision?

A process for making sure you've gathered enough data is the "Four Ws." To discover if you have enough data to address the real need, you should be able to answer each of the "Four W's"—*why, what, when,* and *in what way*:

▶ **Why**—Why is this a problem or concern?

▶ **What**—What do you think is contributing to the problem or concern? What do you need to measure to know if your training solution is addressing the problem?

▶ **When**—When did this problem or concern first start?

▶ **In what way**—How do you recommend you (or your team) address the problem or concern?

It gives you confirmation that you have determined the problem and created the very best solution.

Think About This

Analyzing data is like dating. Sometimes it's an instant connection. The data is straightforward and it just clicks with the problem as described. But, at other times, the connections grow and slowly become apparent. You mull over the data, interpreting and reinterpreting it, and discuss it with colleagues until you're reasonably sure you have a fair assessment of the situation.

Make a Decision

Finally, make a decision. What are you going to recommend and then stand behind? Are you going to decide on an immediate course of action (such as a workshop)? Or are you going to decide on a long-term approach (such as a leadership development program)? Remember, to make the right decision, you need to know

▶ the business challenges to be addressed

▶ the resources available with which to craft a solution.

If you decide that training is the answer, you'll have to decide if you want to build the training or buy it. Then you must determine the best path going forward for creating the optimum training solution within the constraints of time and resources (human, financial, and technical).

If you decide to build, you are choosing to develop your own proprietary sales training courses by leveraging proprietary content, select licensed content, subject matter experts, and other available resources. If you choose to buy, you'll be purchasing or licensing an existing training solution as is, or with some modest tailoring to make it fit your business requirements.

Buying a program generally is done in one of two formats—off-the-shelf and custom outsourcing. If you choose to outsource, you're deciding that bringing in outside resources is a good business decision for your organization; therefore, you must choose how you will leverage outside resources and how you will integrate the outside pieces in your training programs.

There are several things to consider when you're planning to outsource content. Here are the questions to ask:

1. How well does the content of the training map to the knowledge, skills, and abilities you are seeking to teach?
2. How well does the content speak to the business needs and experiences of the full range of your audience?
3. How well does the culture map to the culture you're striving to develop through training?
4. What portion of the content, if any, will you need to "untrain," and how do you do this without undermining the good?
5. In what ways, if any, is the content redundant of, or contradictory to, other content you're using?

When outsourcing trainers or subject matter experts, ask these questions:

1. Does the person bring the depth and breadth of relevant knowledge and experience to be viewed by your audience as a credible facilitator?
2. Does the person have the professional presence and facilitation skills required to meet your delivery standards?
3. Does the person have a professional reputation for maintaining client confidentiality?

When outsourcing technology, ask these questions:

1. Do all of the members of your audience have the ability to access and use the technology?
2. Are there any compatibility issues between the technology to be used and other business systems currently in use?
3. Do you need approval from an information technology officer before deploying this technology?

Considering Alternatives to Classroom Training

Training doesn't necessarily mean creating a full-out formal curriculum. Ask yourself how the required information and skills can be most optimally delivered within the context of your sales training environment, budget, and timing. Several alternative solutions may work:

▶ **Web-based (online) options**—If you find that a salesperson doesn't know how to write proposals, an off-the-shelf online course may give her that knowledge in a straightforward manner.

▶ **Short job aids or sales tools**—If a group is struggling with conveying the benefits of a new product, a quick-reference pocket guide may solve the problem.

▶ **Mentoring or coaching**—In John's case above, there may be an opportunity to have him travel with and be mentored by another sales manager who has overcome the same challenges or is more familiar with the communication styles of John's new customers. This mentor can model the behaviors John needs to adopt and can help him fit more comfortably into his new environment. This approach has a second benefit: It's possible that the time the two salespeople spend together will create a complementary relationship in which each recognizes the strengths of the other and supplies potential leads to the other.

Basic Rule

If you skip a needs assessment in your training preparation, you are placing your most valuable resources at risk, including time to develop the training, time to deliver the training, the productivity of those who attend the training, and the money and talent used to create training materials. All will be wasted if you deliver a training that doesn't respond to the organization's needs.

Targeting the Right Participants

After you've determined that training is the appropriate solution, you have to get the right people to attend. A target audience already has been identified in some cases, but even then you want to ask yourself, Are there others who might benefit from this training? You should also work with the management team to identify the best way to train the right participants. Does the management team need to be trained first? Do you need to roll out a pilot program in one region of the country or the world first? Are top performers expected to attend or can they "test out" of the training? How soon should new hires attend this course? Are new hires within the past year going to benefit from this training?

Editor's Notebook

I constantly have to remind myself to expect that my course participants will join the training already distracted by "more important things they should be doing." When they get there, I'll have a rapidly closing window of opportunity through which to capture their attention and transform these reluctant participants into inspired learners. To do that, I have to make sure I have the right participants in the classroom, and I can build credibility and influence with them through my own competence and skill.

Be careful not to push your training at too many people. There is no greater distraction than participants who think they don't need training, were forced to attend, or just don't know enough to get anything useful from the session.

Use the following simple tactics to ensure that the right salespeople are in your sessions:

▶ **Check your marketing materials for audience descriptions**—Be especially cautious in mentioning an intended skill level (beginner, intermediate, or advanced). One training team described a new class as "geared for seasoned salespeople." Enrollment was huge. But, the team wondered, why was almost no one signing up for the entry-level sales skills class? The simple answer: Everyone identified themselves as "seasoned," no matter how recently they'd started or how poorly they performed. Try to include clear learning objectives and topic descriptions so the learners know what to expect.

Basic Rule

Training isn't always the answer. When it isn't, be prepared to explain why and to offer alternative solutions to the issue at hand.

▶ **Engage your enrollees before the training**—Salespeople want interaction and they love to talk about themselves. Contact them before the training and ask them a few of the questions below:

1. What are you most looking forward to during class?
2. Why are you coming to training?
3. How would you describe yourself in 15 seconds or less?
4. What do you like best about your position?
5. What are your greatest challenges?

This pre-training contact enables you to learn about the people you'll be training before they arrive at the training room. If you grow concerned that they may be enrolled in the wrong training, you can offer alternatives before their time is poorly spent.

Drawing Up a Written Training Contract

Ultimately, a needs analysis should be treated as a contract. The person requesting the training should receive a clear definition of what you're delivering. Likewise, you should have a clear description of the requestor's desired outcome(s). The contract spells out for all parties what should and should not be expected, and it ensures these details are mutually agreed up front.

Treating the training arrangements with an official document sets the tone for the training event itself and establishes conditions against which to measure its success afterward. The purpose of a needs assessment contract is to state as fully as possible the existing situation and the desired outcome.

Tool 5-2 is a foundation on which you can build a basic training contract. This tool is intended as a starting point. Adjust and customize its elements for your own purposes. The items presented in the various sections will prompt you to seek the descriptive information you need to fully understand the training request, the anticipated outcomes, and the measurements that will be used in judging its ultimate success. After consulting with the business area leader or project sponsor who has made the training request, be sure you record all pertinent information on this part of the training contract.

Tool 5-2. Training Contract, Sections Describing Issue, Training Requested, and Desired Outcomes

Customer Profile

Who is the lead training developer?

Who are the training development team members?

What business area(s) is (are) affected?

Who is the business area contact (or project sponsor)?

What is the date of training request?

continued on next page

Tool 5-2. Training Contract, Sections Describing Issue, Training Requested, and Desired Outcomes (continued)

Current Situation

What are the business goals to which the training topic links?

What are the corporate goals to which the training topic links?

What are the current gaps (what is missing in the process or procedure)?

What is the current impact on productivity, job performance, and efficiency?

What is the period of time this situation has been occurring?

What are the "work-arounds" currently in place to address this issue?

What are the reports currently required, including the nature of data collected and people to whom reports are submitted?

Situation/Department Background

What are the learners' names, length of time on the job, focus tasks/procedures, work locations, and so forth?

What are the other attempts to address this issue (what was done, when, by whom, and the result/reaction)?

What employees previously received training related to the issue/topic, including details of the training and when it occurred?

What are the current means of measuring job performance, including standards and frequency of measurement?

What options other than training have been considered to
address this need?

What business variables could affect the project timeline,
final product, or development process?

What are the plans for addressing those variables?

Expected Performance Outcomes

What are the specific productivity improvements the
sponsor would like to see?

What are the documented business issues motivating this
training request?

What are the performance improvements or behavior
changes that the business expects as a result of the training being requested?

Outcome Metrics

How will return-on-investment be determined; what are
the criteria to be used by area leadership to determine
training's success?

What is current status or established baseline against
which progress will be measured, and what is the
expected level of improvement as a result of training?

The training project contract should contain the following information:

▶ a summary review of the stated need and the current situation
▶ fact-based declaration of training as the appropriate solution
▶ overview of the proposed training plan (including relevant development and
approval milestones)
▶ detailed description of training delivery (delivery method, content, target
audience, agenda with timeline, and any needed "customized" training for
targeted teams)

▶ *(very important)* organizational resources that are required to support you as you work to complete the project—the kinds of things without which your development progress would be severely hampered

▶ signatures of all parties involved.

When the contract has been completed in detail and signed by the business leader and the training department, everyone will have signed off officially on both the recap of the need and the proposed solution.

Getting It Done

Use these questions for a training you have been asked to provide. They will help you identify prospective learners' needs and help you create an effective training result:

1. What is the business-based problem you hope to solve?
2. What is the greatest challenge the prospective learners have at the moment?
3. What benefits will participants attain by attending training?
4. What are the ideal behaviors you hope to see exhibited and measured as a result of training?
5. What challenges may need to be anticipated and overcome in preparing or delivering the training?
6. What are the consequences to participants if their behaviors don't change?

For the same proposed training, complete the work plan presented in tool 5-1.

Phase 3: Enabling Sales Team Learning

Carol A. Dawson

■ ■

What's Inside This Chapter

In this chapter, you'll learn

▶ The definition of blended learning
▶ The benefits of using blended learning
▶ How to incorporate a variety of electronic tools in your training.

If they're going to learn, retain, and successfully apply the knowledge and skills improvement you offer in training, salespeople need stimulating and relevant activities both inside and outside the classroom. Providing multiple learning pathways is just good business for your training team.

For example, web-based courses offer salespeople greater and more timely access to needed information. Having content available online makes it easy for learners to complete some or all of the work on their own time, when they find it more convenient. Salespeople often keep crazy schedules. Many work early in the morning and well into the night.

Tech-based or computer-aided training that's ready when they need it and when they can clear away distractions and concentrate on it offers an excellent just-in-time training experience. It's less stressful for the learners because its opportunity costs are reduced.

Blended learning involves more than one content delivery pathway in a training situation. For example, a course may include a computer-based training module that participants complete on their own, as well as a discussion board in which participants collaborate with others. Another course may require that learners read a book or article to supplement their "synchronous learning event" (an online class with an instructor making a presentation in real time).

Blended learning gives your learners various avenues to get information they need at the time they need it. Here's an example: After a classroom or online training session addressing ways to handle difficult customers, ask your learners to watch a video clip that portrays a scenario involving a difficult customer. Post questions on a discussion board (I'll describe discussion boards later in the chapter), and ask learners to post their responses. You might ask these questions:

▶ What did the salesperson do correctly in this scenario?
▶ How could the salesperson have been more effective?
▶ What was the customer's response to the salesperson's approach?

Creating this type of interactive and interpersonal environment enables learners to respond to your pertinent questions and to read and comment on other participants' responses. It expands and reinforces the learning.

Another way to reinforce learning is to give job aids to your salesforce. For example, if a sales rep needs to be able to demonstrate how a new product works, prepare a short video clip to explain the product's features and function.

The more ways in which you engage learners with the content, the more likely they are to learn and retain it. For example, a person learning a new computer system might do any or all of the following things:

▶ listen to an instructor lecture
▶ read a manual

▶ watch someone demonstrate how to do specific functions
▶ practice in a training class.

The more of those things the learner does, the more likely she or he is to remember how to use the system on the job. Approaching and repeating content through various sensory and thought-process forms of presentation increase retention.

Traditionally, when a new product or service was ready to launch, it was common practice for a business to gather its entire salesforce at headquarters to learn the new item's features, benefits, and details. With a widely dispersed sales corps, this effort cost a fortune in both money and time. It wasn't the most efficient use of resources, but there were no options.

Those days are gone. Technology equips us now to communicate in person, in real time, over enormous distances. And tech-based blended learning offers us a cache of options for sharing knowledge when training doesn't require a face-to-face experience. The salesperson invests less time in travel outside his or her territory. The company invests fewer financial resources in moving its employees from field to classroom. The training department is recognized as a solution provider, which reinforces its value in the eyes of the organization. Everyone wins!

Noted

We are, as a species, blended learners.
—Elliot Masie, analyst and learning researcher

In this chapter, you'll learn about several ways you can enhance (or replace) your classroom training and wow your trainees with interactive and meaningful content. We'll start with a review of the benefits of this approach, and then we'll go into detail on a number of tech-based methods for sharing knowledge and improving skills.

Tools at Your Disposal
Face-to-face instruction is still a major component of most sales training programs. However, a number of blended learning tools are useful in supplementing face-to-

face instruction, or even replacing it in some situations. Here, I'll show you how to get started with the following tools:

▶ webinars

▶ synchronous e-learning

▶ asynchronous e-learning

▶ mobile content

▶ wikis and discussion boards

▶ blogs.

Webinars

Webinars (web-based seminars) are meetings convened via the Internet. A presenter delivers a lecture or conducts a demonstration in real time while others view the presentation online. Participants are able to talk with each other and with the presenter via standard phone lines or by Voice over Internet protocol (usually referred to as "VoIP"), where the call is made through the computer. This is basically the same setup as that used for synchronous learning events, which will be discussed next. Despite the chance for two-way communication, however, webinars tend to be mainly monologues, with the presenter doing most of the talking.

You may want to use webinars to do any of the following things:

▶ Demonstrate how to use a product or service.

▶ Provide your customers with free information on a topic they'll find valuable to draw them to your other services. For example, a company specializing in presentation skills and other types of communication might offer a free webinar on writing effective emails, and then include information about its paid courses.

▶ Explain and demonstrate a new procedure to your salesforce.

▶ Bring new sales reps up to speed on company policies, history, and processes: HR practices, general benefits information, a tour of the company website. This is especially useful for new employees who live some distance from a company office.

To get started sign up for a web conferencing platform. (See the "Resources" section at the back of the book.) There is a cost involved in hosting webinars and synchronous learning events. Our online meeting vendor charges a flat monthly fee for each person who has an account, but access is unlimited. You also will have a separate charge, whether through your online meeting vendor or your telephone service provider, for the teleconference portion. Typically, it's a per-person, per-minute charge. For example, if the cost is three cents a minute for each person, a one-hour webinar for 20 people, including the facilitator, would cost $36.00 ($1.80 per person).

When you have management's approval to use webinars and have chosen a vendor, visit your vendor's website for instructions on how to set up your account. You likely will be given a user name and password. Your vendor should provide training on the use of its software to create classes. In general, you'll set up your class ahead of time, invite your participants, and give them a link to the meeting.

Start your meeting about 30 minutes prior to your session's start time. You'll need this time to load your documents and get the teleconference set up. Be prepared to welcome those who link in early.

Depending on your vendors for your web hosting and learning management system (LMS), you may be able to link them together so you can start your web classes from your LMS. This will require the involvement of your information technology department.

If webinars are new to your company, you'll do a lot of ad hoc training to get your people comfortable using the technology. Give pre-session tutorials on how to use the tools that you'll be using that day—polling, chat, raised hand, and writing on the screen. If this is your first session, log on and do a few practice meetings so you're comfortable using the tools yourself. This is one of the benefits of paying a flat monthly fee; it costs you nothing to practice.

Noted

You learn something every day if you pay attention.
—Ray LeBlond, director of corporate development and communications, Tourism British Columbia

If possible, make use of a producer—a person who can help participants get into the session, watch the chat for questions, add a second voice to the call, and generally help you manage the details. When I first began doing web-based training and didn't have a producer, I had to stop the class if someone was having trouble getting linked in. A few experiences like that convinced me to bring in an associate.

Typically, you'll have several options for what you can share in an online meeting. You can import documents that can be viewed through the meeting interface. Be careful about videos; you may need special software from your online meeting vendor to enable participants to view the videos. Also be cautious if you are using advanced functions in your PowerPoint slides. Animations will work one at a time within the online meeting software. If you have created animations in which you click one image and something else happens, they won't work within the meeting tool. To make them work properly, you'll need to share your desktop and then pull up the presentation.

Important note: Disable your email and any chat functions you have before sharing your desktop. I once watched an online software demonstration where a friend of the presenter started a chat swearing and talking about someone else. You do not want this to happen to you.

Sharing your desktop is also helpful if you want to demonstrate a process or software program. For example, if you intend to demonstrate how to use a database for tracking sales numbers, you can't import the database into your meeting.

You can share web content by going directly to a website. This is particularly helpful if you're going to demonstrate the functionality of your website for new customers or new employees.

A whiteboard is an interactive tool you can use in a webinar. It gives you a white screen where you can allow participants to draw freehand or type directly. Turning on this feature before the session starts lets your participants type and draw for practice. Imagine that you're the marketing director of a large men's clothing company, and you want to solicit your sales reps' ideas on how to release a new line of raincoats. Your salesforce is situated along the mid-Atlantic coast, so you opt for an online meeting. Instead of getting right to the questions you hope will elicit information you can use in designing the marketing strategy, you ask participants to spend five minutes drawing on their whiteboards. They don't have to draw raincoats—they don't have to draw anything identifiable. The value of the exercise isn't in the picture; it's in the act of drawing. They're accessing the creativity centers of their brains. With those centers open and active, the sales reps are much more likely to come up with new ideas—ideas that would not have been generated without the drawing lead-in to creativity. If you do encourage them to draw or write something related to the session's topic, you focus their creativity before the session gets under way.

Be sure to explore all the meeting options your vendor provides. You should be able to let your participants do the following:

▶ Use the drawing tools.

▶ Chat with each other directly. (*Note: Use this with caution.*)

Editor's Notebook

My organization decided to roll out a training initiative via webinar. To save the cost of hundreds of associates traveling to a central location, we created a 20-minute web-based training module and sent its link to our target audience.

To create the module, we built a PowerPoint presentation with screen shots of a new process being implemented. Then the subject matter expert and I sat in a room and narrated each slide, using a microphone and Fugent Publisher software. It took about half a day to record the narration.

When the recording was done, we used Publisher software to upload it to the Fugent website, where it was converted into a flash file and assigned a URL. As part of that process, we were able to indicate what information we wanted to gather from our viewers before anyone watched the module. We collected key data, such as associate identification number, first name, user name, and so forth, so we could track who had accessed the module. When those data had been collected, we would create a report to show managers which of their associates had accessed the training module, how many slides they viewed, and how much time they spent in the module.

Our original plan to conduct this training initiative for several hundred associates across the United States involved hosting a number of conference calls with different audiences— a process that would have cost thousands of dollars in time, teleconference fees, travel expenses, and trainer salaries. When we revamped the plan into a webinar, we cut our costs to only the time and salary it took to prepare the PowerPoint presentation and record the audio portion.

The webinar was a great success, and the same audience asked that other trainings be provided in the same way—thus saving the company even more time and money where travel and teleconferences had previously been the norm.

▶ View any document. This is helpful if you want to have different people typing on different screens at the same time. For example, imagine that you're teaching sales managers how to motivate their pharmaceutical sales reps to increase their repeat-customer percentages. You divide the full group of participants into three smaller groups, and then assign different whiteboards and tasks to each group:

> ▶ whiteboard 1: list the challenges to getting repeat customers
> ▶ whiteboard 2: list tips for encouraging repeat business
> ▶ whiteboard 3: list the benefits to repeat business.

Then, as a full group, you talk through the list on each of the whiteboards.

▶ View any page of the document being discussed. This is helpful for participants who missed something you said and want to go back without interrupting you. Remember, however, that this also enables learners to look ahead.

Synchronous E-Learning

Synchronous learning events are somewhat similar to webinars, but there are several important distinctions. As in webinars, all participants are collaborating at the same time ("synchronously"). Whereas webinars usually have one or a few people giving information to the participants and offering few opportunities for dialogue, synchronous learning events involve the learner in the process.

Well before your session starts, build your class in PowerPoint. You can import the PowerPoint presentation into the online tool when it's time to host the class. Include a welcome screen with the title of the class, as well as the teleconference number and passcode, if you're using one. To personalize the experience for your distance learners, follow the title welcome screen with a picture of you (and of your producer, if you're using one).

Include a slide of "housekeeping" items. Not everyone has participated in an online class before, so it's helpful to give the following instructions before the session begins:

▶ Explain how to mute the phone, and when muting should be used.
▶ Tell participants not to put the group on hold, because it leaves the group listening to music until the person who pressed "hold" returns.
▶ Explain what to do if the computer goes to sleep.
▶ Describe how to use all of the tools you'll need for that session, including the toolbar, the chat panel, polling, and the raise-hand function.

When those instructions are complete, begin your topic presentation.

Remember a few basic rules about using PowerPoint slides on the web:

▶ Use a light background with dark text. In the online environment, light type on a dark ground often seems to shimmer and may be difficult to read.

▶ Avoid combining red and green items on a slide or creating layouts where you must refer to "the red box" or "the green numbers," for example. People with red-green color blindness will have problems distinguishing those items.

▶ Leave a lot of white space (open space with no type or image) on the screen. Don't overdo the text. That is probably the most common complaint about presentations done for classroom audiences, and it carries over to online classes as well. A key graphic and a couple bullet points are all you need on each slide; then you can talk about the details and expand on the topic.

Think About This

Here is the technology you'll need for webinars and synchronous learning events:

- *Internet access, preferably high-speed access*
- *a conference call vendor that allows for multiple phone lines or VoIP technology*
- *a vendor for your web-based platform, such as WebEx or GoToMeeting. (See the "Resources" section for links.)*

In my online classes, participants have outside reading assignments each week, and we meet online to review what they've read and to apply it through discussion, case study, and other activities.

Online meeting software includes tools that participants can control with a mouse—such as a pen that lets them draw freehand—and a tool that places rectangles, circles, and other shapes on the screen. Using these tools, you and the participants can draw pictures, type text into shaped boxes on the electronic whiteboard that appears on every screen (rather like a classroom flip chart).

As mentioned in the earlier discussion of webinars, online meeting software used for synchronous learning events enables learners to talk with the presenter and with one another. Participants either dial into a conference call or they use VoIP on the computers. VoIP requires that each participant have headphones and a built-in microphone. Using the phone capabilities offered through your meeting software tends to be more expensive than using a stand-alone teleconference service. This is partly because the software generally is operator-assisted. If you have a large number of participants joining a session, however, the assistance may be worth the cost.

Editor's Notebook

My favorite way to use whiteboards is to open them up before my synchronous learning events begin and let participants draw whatever they like there (as long as it's appropriate for the office environment). This is a great way to personalize the experience for everyone, to let people introduce themselves, and to get all the creative juices running.

To do this, I start my online training classes about 15 minutes ahead of schedule and turn on the annotation tools for the participants. I sometimes prime the pump by drawing one of the few things I can draw: stick people, smiley faces, or pine trees. I'm also on the phone at this time, encouraging others to join in the fun and praising the participants' drawings.

When it's time to begin the session, I switch to the actual presentation. Although during the session we generally don't revisit what the participants have written or drawn on the whiteboard, I sometimes leave it open. The exercise relaxes and prepares trainees to take an active part in the session.

A distinction between synchronous e-learning and webinars is the use of printed participant guides. Whereas webinars tend not to use them, synchronous events usually do. Participants having a guide at hand during the learning usually find it easier to follow along with the onscreen presentations, and if you run short of time before you've covered all of the content, the concepts are there in the guide for learners to review on their own.

Some facilitators will simply print their PowerPoint slides as a participant guide, three slides to a page with space or faint lines off to the side for notes. If you think such handouts might work for your class, here are two issues to consider first:

▶ Participants can preview everything before you present it (including answers to built-in quizzes). It may be more useful to remove the details from your slide printouts. In place of key words or phrases, insert blank lines.

► If you have layered animations on your slides, they will print on top of each other and be unreadable.

At the beginning of the participant guide, give all the details of your online meeting, including the web link to the session, the teleconference information, and information on how learners may contact you if they have questions.

Distribute your participant materials before the class. At least a week ahead of time is best, but not always feasible. You might make them available for downloading at a website, include them with the class invitation, or email them to those who sign up. If the guides are sent electronically, make it clear that learners need to print them before joining the class. In case they don't do the printing, your online meeting software may offer you the ability to make the guide available after the session has started.

Asynchronous E-Learning

Asynchronous e-learning is also referred to as "computer-based training." With this type of instructional pathway, trainers and participants don't meet at a scheduled time. Instead, the trainer creates a content module, using an e-learning authoring tool, and then posts the module online. Several authoring tools are available: Adobe Captivate, CourseLab, Articulate, and Lectora, for example. Learners complete the modules at their own workstations and at their own pace.

Questions and collaboration are possible with asynchronous learning, but not in real time. You might make yourself available at set times, via phone or email, to respond to their queries. Or you might set up a discussion board (discussed later in this chapter) where students post questions. Engage a subject matter expert to answer those questions on the board. In that way, people who may have the same question will find the answer waiting for them.

If you prepare a participant guide, make it accessible through the module. Do that by putting a link to the guide at the beginning of your module. The specific authoring software you use will dictate the process for creating the link.

There are several advantages to using asynchronous e-learning:

► No face-to-face instruction is required. When the module is created, it can be used repeatedly with little or no input from the instructor.
► Participants can access content when it's convenient for them. This is particularly helpful in customer-facing environments, where being responsive to customer needs may discourage classroom instruction.

▶ Assessments can be built into the modules to enable students to self-check their progress. You also may be able to check the results of your learners' sessions, depending on how the module is built and how it interacts with your learning management system. Some authoring software will allow results to be emailed to you. Of course, if you have a great number of trainees taking the course, that may not be a good choice. Another option is to direct score reports to the learning management system, where you or someone else with access to the system may monitor progress. On a recent module I built, 70 percent was the minimum passing score. If a learner didn't achieve that score, the module automatically returned to the beginning. Then the student could navigate to any screen and look at the material she or he had missed.

Although asynchronous courses provide flexibility for the learner, here are a couple things you should consider before you choose them for your training:

▶ There is no live instructor available, so you must create a process for participants to get their questions answered.
▶ Computer-based training modules require at least as much development time as a face-to-face event, if not more.

The key with this type of learning is to remember that in its purest form, asynchronous learning is "learning without direct interaction with an instructor." The key challenge to overcome when using this modality is to remember to develop a course that can satisfy all learning types.

For example, if a person is listening to a new product launch podcast and has a question, that question goes unanswered. Or, if someone is participating in a self-paced tutorial and gets stuck (either instructionally or technologically), the learning is replaced by something that's always ready and waiting—real work. So, you must develop asynchronous learning with these considerations in mind. That's why asynchronous learning fits well into a blended learning approach. The learner can do some learning when it's convenient, but still has access to interaction and support.

Mobile Content

Mobile content is just that—it's portable so learners can take it with them instead of being tied to a desk or a classroom. It can turn a personal digital assistant (PDA), a digital music player, a handheld game console, or a mobile phone into a classroom.

Think About This

- In 2010, Generation Y will outnumber Baby Boomers. Ninety-six percent of them have joined a social network (Grunwald Associates National Study).
- One out of eight couples married in the United States in 2008 met via social media (Huffington Post).
- Years to reach 50 million users: radio 38, TV 13, Internet 4, iPod 3. Facebook added 100 million users in less than nine months. iPhone applications hit 1 billion in nine months (United Nations Cyberschoolbus; Mashable Social Media Guide; Apple).
- If Facebook were a country, it would be the world's fourth largest, situated between the United States and Indonesia. And its population is growing— Facebook recently announced 300 million users.

Podcasts are audio or video digital media files distributed over the Internet by syndicated download, through web feeds, to portable media players and personal computers. This downloading is accomplished through "Really Simple Syndication" (or RSS).

A popular source for podcasts is Apple's iTunes Store. Its content has grown exponentially over the last couple years, and many universities are making free content available there. Podcasts can be downloaded and listened to on any portable iPod or MP3 player, or directly through your desktop computer's speakers.

Portable content opens a world of possibilities for organizations and learners alike. Here are some examples:

▶ There's a TV commercial advertising a guided cooking tutorial that's played on a handheld game console. While cooking a new dish, you can watch a video showing how to prepare it, stopping and restarting the tutorial as you go through the process.

▶ A Hilton Hotel in Phoenix, Arizona, uses iPods to train housekeepers on every procedure they must perform to clean and prepare rooms for hotel guests. The company training goals were to provide consistency in knowledge and performance, and to overcome language-barrier problems that members of the housekeeping staff were experiencing. Previous training videos, prepared in English and Spanish, had been costly to produce. Switching to video podcasts has cut the costs considerably. These podcasts use no words. Instead, trainees navigate through the information by following two-dimensional icons and three-dimensional animations. Because each step is vividly demonstrated in pictures, no words are needed.

▶ Some zoos and museums are using iPods, rather than human tour guides and docents, to guide visitors through their exhibits. Visitors move at their own pace and can skip or replay portions of the podcast.

▶ Learners now have access to a huge variety of tutorials covering topics from new languages to product demonstrations.

▶ iTunes has quite a few sales podcasts available, free of charge. Visit the iTunes Store online (http://www.itunes.com) and type "sales training" in the search box. Click "Podcasts" on the left navigation panel, and click "See All."

Here are some uses for mobile learning:

▶ Step-by-step tutorials your salesforce can use to show potential customers the key features of your company's products or services

▶ daily motivational messages for your sales staff

▶ success stories explaining or showing how other salespeople implemented a recent initiative.

To start audio podcasting (that is, without video), you'll need the following tools:

▶ *Recording software:* There are free tools available that do a great job (for example, Audacity). If you use a Mac platform, iLife comes with a podcasting tool. (See the "Resources" section for links.)

▶ *Headset with a microphone:* Get one that connects to your computer. There are lots of good ones on the market and you can get a decent one for $30–$40.

▶ *Server to store the file:* Most likely, your company will require that you keep your podcast files on the company intranet so they are not available to the public.

Although mobile learning has revolutionized how training is made available and accessed, there are some concerns that need to be addressed. Here are some examples:

▶ A learner's ability to access content will depend on having an Internet connection.

▶ The battery life of the learner's mobile device may be an issue for longer training modules. When you have a lot of content, make several smaller modules rather than one long one.

▶ Screen resolution of video podcasts must support the smaller screen sizes on mobile devices.

▶ Screen and key sizes may make reading the content and navigating the module difficult on handheld devices.

Carefully consider those factors when deciding to incorporate mobile content in your training program. Not paying attention to them may result in a really great training course that your audience can't use.

Wikis and Discussion Boards

"Wiki" is the Hawaiian word for "quick." In our present context, the word refers to a website that enables dispersed people to collaborate on content. They can input, edit, and delete content (their own and that of others). The online encyclopedia Wikipedia is the obvious example of this technology.

Wikis are helpful when two or more people are working on a project. Pages can be assigned to each type of content; calendars and other widgets (mini-applications) can be added; and, for a monthly fee, some wikis can be made private so only those who are invited can view the content. Wikis are especially helpful in on-the-job training or in-the-field sales contests. People can get and add sales tips and can update their personal progress in a competition. Content is updated in real time. Everyone participating has access to the most current information.

To set up your own wiki, you'll need an account with a provider. One popular provider is www.wikispaces.com. Once you have an account, you can create as many different wikis as you like. Each wiki offers different levels of access, and you probably will want to choose one that is private. It will cost a small amount that you'll pay monthly or yearly.

Wikis generally have discussion boards (but you don't need a wiki to have a discussion board). A discussion board is an online bulletin board on which people can post their comments, questions, concerns, thoughts, or issues. A discussion board may be very generic or related to a specific process, topic, or product. When a discussion "thread" (string of comments posted) is started by one person typing a question or comment on the board, others can reply to it immediately.

For example, if you type a question about a particular product, someone who knows the answer can respond. When that thread exists, someone else with the same question can search for an answer, see the original thread, and use the answer. Others also can reply to an existing thread or start one of their own on the same discussion board. Most boards require that readers register to get access to the website and to post a comment; registration generally is free.

A discussion board also may be a good "train-the-trainer" resource. You might combine it with a wiki where you and your training colleagues share all the things you've learned about training technologies, presentation skills, what have you. Such a dynamic compendium of information will be valuable, no matter the size of your organization.

The users of wikis and discussion boards generate content, so some amount of caution and oversight is necessary. Because anyone can add content, you may run into incorrect information or some content that you don't want to see or distribute. The person who sets up the wiki or board will be its administrator and may appoint others to monitor the use of these tools, correct inaccurate information, remove inappropriate content, and ban abusive users when necessary.

Blogs

The word "blog" is short for "web log." Basically, a blog is an online journal that others can read. There are blogs on every topic imaginable. To see it for yourself, just type a topic into your search engine, add the word "blog" after the topic, and look out. There's a flood coming!

For people interested in training, a good blog is the Rapid eLearning Blog (http://www.articulate.com/rapid-elearning), where the blog's author shares ideas and hints for quickly creating e-learning courses. It's one of my favorite sources of inspiration when I'm designing courses, whether live or online.

Another blog resource is the Blog Catalog (www.blogcatalog.com). This site will direct you to a number of sales-related blogs; in fact, as I write this, I see there are 1,459 of them. When you get to the site, type "sales" in the search box and look for blogs that relate to topics you want to view. There are blogs about motivation, marketing, real estate sales, effective selling—and the list goes on.

Blogs can be very useful tools for communicating with your audience and can help build a sense of community. Here are a few ideas for using a blog in the training context:

- to offer tips to new sales associates
- to encourage and motivate the salesforce
- to share sales managers' ideas on how to lead a salesforce
- to explain the benefits of your product or service.

To start your own blog, go to a blog-hosting site, such as www.blogger.com. Follow the directions for setting up a free account. You will have to sign up for a free Google account, if you don't already have one. Choose a name for your blog that will help your audience identify it—perhaps something like *Sales Training for Busy Reps*. You'll also choose a URL for your blog; keep it short and simple so it's easy to remember and type.

When you've completed the setup process, it's time to start writing. Here are some guidelines:

- Keep your individual posts fairly short (250–500 words) and conversational in tone. Don't fill them with technical jargon. It will help your readers if you stick to one subject in each post. This will increase the likelihood that they'll continue to read what you're writing.
- Use proper grammar, punctuation, and sentence structure to make reading and understanding your ideas much easier.
- Provide links to other resources that your readers will find helpful. If you have a blog for salespeople, include links to websites that help them improve their sales techniques or enhance their time management skills. Use keywords in your posts so people can find your blog when they type that keyword into a search engine.
- Be very careful with what you say in your blog. Many people use these online journals to let off steam or share their viewpoints. Remember that your posts are visible. When you publish them, they can't be retracted. Even if you're able to remove the entry, you have no idea who already has seen and perhaps printed it. A few words of frustration can come back to haunt you. Bloggers are being served with lawsuits, and the trend is likely to grow as lawsuits are won against bloggers who step outside the bounds of common sense.

Getting It Done

Now that you know something about an array of tools that can diversify and extend the reach of your training, it's time to imagine real-world ways you can apply these technologies in your training department. For each of the tools listed below, brainstorm two ideas for using them in your own company.

Webinars

1. _____

2. _____

Synchronous e-learning

1. _____

2. _____

Asynchronous e-learning

1. _____

2. _____

Mobile content

1. _____

2. _____

Wikis

1. _____

2. _____

Discussion boards

1. _____

2. _____

Blogs

1. _____

2. _____

Phase 4: Executing Your Value-Added Solution

Renie McClay

■ ■

What's Inside This Chapter

In this chapter, you'll learn

▶ Valuable time-saving and organizational skills for the classroom
▶ Inspirational ideas to motivate and engage your participants
▶ Alternative approaches to delivering sales content.

With your training designed and your classroom environment prepared, it's time to jump in and deliver the goods. For people who haven't been involved in training, games and activities may seem like pointless fun. But as a trainer, you know their importance in learning. Games, exercises, contests, and small- or large-group activities energize and involve learners in ways that few PowerPoint presentations and lectures ever will.

And now consider the special challenges your learners present! With a group of salespeople, these experiences are even more crucial. You're delivering training to an audience who needs a lot of stimulation, participation, and movement during your sessions.

In a classroom setting, salespeople are often antsy, distracted, and bored. They aren't accustomed to sitting for long periods of time, rarely spend time in the office, and don't have the tolerance for content that won't help them sell more and better now. You must move them constantly, and must keep shifting gear to ensure that you're holding their attention and that learning is happening—all while making the training fun and enjoyable. You must keep reminding them how they can use what you're teaching them in the classroom when they're back in the field.

Noted

Price is what you pay. Value is what you get.
—Warren Buffett, American investment entrepreneur

Of course, no trainer wants to put his audience to sleep or waste his attendees' time but the pressure to produce value for time spent is particularly strong on sales trainers. Planning and preparation get you part of the way to that value; delivering the training is where it comes together and either succeeds or falls flat.

Throughout this chapter, we'll concentrate on ways you can make your training more interesting and engaging for your uniquely demanding learners.

Get Your Learners Engaged

Extensive research has been done to prove the critical significance of participant engagement and interaction in a learning experience. When you engage your participants with activities, you give them the valuable opportunity to use new knowledge and practice new techniques and skills in a safe environment. This is key for salespeople because they need continuous stimuli to keep them motivated to learn.

It's an added benefit that classroom interactions prompt people to learn from each other. Interaction and mutual learning help reinforce what's being taught because they present the topics from various perspectives and in diverse ways.

Experts have shown that the average participant exposed only one time to a new concept has a retention rate of about 10 percent. However, if the trainer can drive a concept or reinforce a point at least six additional times within during the course, the participant's retention may increase to 90 percent!

Editor's Notebook

Using Color in Your Classroom

In his book The Power of Color *(1991), Morton Walker discusses the influence that color has on learning. Although it usually is beyond your reach in a training room to choose the color of your walls or the shade of desks and carpet, you can use color to stimulate learning in a variety of other ways. Consider the colors of the clothes you wear; table coverings, name tent cards, and binder and participant guide covers; posters you hang, handouts you distribute, and PowerPoint slides you show; and the baskets and bins placed on tables to hold gadgets, markers, sticky notes—and candy.*

Let's examine some colors:

- **Red** *is an engaging color. It's considered more disturbing by people who tend to be anxious, and more exciting to people who are calm.*
- **Yellow** *is the first color a person distinguishes in the brain. Often associated with stress and caution, it also can stimulate an overall sense of optimism, hope, and balance.*
- **Orange** *combines the impressions of red and yellow. It sparks energy and creativity.*
- **Blue** *is the most tranquil color. It calms us and increases feelings of well-being. When we see blue, the brain releases 11 neurotransmitters that relax the body. In a classroom setting, it may be a bit too calming.*
- **Green** *evokes a sense of calm.*
- **Brown** *promotes a sense of security and relaxation, and it reduces fatigue.*

Have a Plan

Preparation and excellent time management are a must in delivering any training. A lack of preparation shows through in your delivery, and your participants most certainly will catch on. Don't let your lack of planning interfere with what would otherwise be a great session.

When planning for your training events, apply basic meeting management processes. Just like meetings, every training event should include a purpose, an agenda, and a timeframe.

Craft your agenda with these tips in mind:

▶ Plan your content to take 15 minutes less than the time you've allotted for your training session. For example, if you have a one-hour training session scheduled, plan only 45 minutes of content. No one wants to be kept longer than she expects.

▶ Create two agendas—one for you, with specific timeframes for every topic and activity clearly stated, and one for your audience, with topics and presenters identified but only start and end times for the entire training session listed. If you have to adjust on the fly, it's easier to do that without everyone in your audience knowing what they may have missed.

▶ Give plenty of breaks. A 10-minute break every two hours is the minimum.

▶ Start and end on time. If you don't stay mindful of the clock, you appear not to respect your participants' time. With that reputation, you may find it tough to getting recurrent participation.

Basic Rule

Allow time on the agenda for salespeople to return phone calls and follow up on email. It will help them stay focused on the training content and will reduce their anxiety about what must be done.

Preplanning from start to finish helps you present a professional training event, eases anxiety, and enables you to focus on your participants. Spend some time taking care of all the details—printing materials, assembling handouts, planning refreshments and logistics, and so forth. This is where most instructors fail, and why they look unorganized during their training sessions.

What to Cover Before Launching into Your Content

When everyone is seated, and before you begin the training itself, address the following topics:

Think About This

Never keep participants longer than stated on the agenda! Participants won't remember how dynamic you were or how much they learned—but they will remember that you held them hostage in class.

▶ **Preview break times**—Letting participants know when they'll be able to take short breaks and when they'll be expected back in the classroom is a good way to keep to the schedule. At the beginning of the class, tell them

  ▶ when they'll get breaks, and how long the breaks will be
  ▶ if and when they'll have additional time to return calls and check email.

This is crucial for salespeople. If you can accommodate one or two chunks of time in the agenda, do it! Your learners will thank you and will be able to stay more focused on the training.

Basic Rule

When you set clear expectations, you eliminate unnecessary distractions.

▶ **Establish ground rules**—These are the rules your group will live by during the training session(s). It's a good idea to present them and get participant agreement at the beginning of the training. The rules will help you facilitate the class and ensure you stay on track. When you present your list of ground rules, ask if everyone can live with them. If the group can't, you'll need to address the problem. Either clarify the item in question or strike it from the list. Use your ground rules as a reference when they're violated, but you can do so only if you've gotten buy-in up front. Here's a list of possible ground rules:

  ▶ Sessions and breaks will start and end on time.
  ▶ Cell phones/PDAs will be put on vibrate mode or be turned off.
  ▶ There will be no email exchanges during class.

▷ No one will have side conversations. If it's pertinent to the topic, it should be shared.

▷ We agree to disagree.

▷ We respect one another.

▷ **Create an issues board**—Many call this a "parking lot." With salespeople, it's nonnegotiable! Participants have 100 things running through their heads at the same moment, and one discussion will spark dozens of questions or ideas. The issues board is a place for them to note those questions and ideas without disturbing the flow of presentation or discussion. Put pads of sticky-notes on the tables, and instruct learners to jot down whatever issues come to mind and place the notes on a flip chart or whiteboard during class breaks. Check the board to identify answers to their questions or get the group involved and start a discussion.

Think About This

Keep track of the items that are placed on the issue board from class to class. This will help you gauge which topics are mentioned most frequently and might warrant inclusion in the agenda.

Games and Activities to Use

It takes creative thinking to get salespeople pumped up to learn about prospecting, identifying decision makers, defining problems needing solutions, overcoming objections, selling more, and the like. If you don't consider yourself creative, don't worry. Use your resources! You have a plethora of people around you who can help you design your activities.

Don't let time constraints get in the way of activities you think will benefit your learners. Instead, choose your activities first and set your content agenda around them. Identify the knowledge or skill that your salespeople absolutely need to have when the session is over, choose one or more activities that will present and reinforce that information or skill, and then allot the rest of your time to additional content activities that solidify the learning.

The following activities will help reinforce the most important information you're offering your salespeople by letting you revisit those topics you've covered already:

- ▶ role play
- ▶ review games and quizzes
- ▶ case studies
- ▶ mock trials and debates
- ▶ improvisation
- ▶ storytelling.

Using activities increases group involvement, enhances retention, reinforces an application, and provides nonthreatening practice opportunities. It also addresses a variety of learning styles. Adults learn in a number of ways. Some people favor auditory input; some prefer visual or kinesthetic learning through sight or movement. One of your training challenges is to meet all of your participants' learning needs by offering something for every learning style. Incorporate activities that stimulate learners in a variety of ways.

Think About This

Activities serve a significant purpose in your sessions. They spur participation, prompt discussion, and open a forum for sharing common experiences. The pacing of these activities should be set by the participants.

In the rest of this section, we'll take an in-depth look at several of the activities you'll find useful in presenting knowledge, introducing and developing your participants' skills, and reinforcing content in a way that boosts their after-class retention and beneficial use of the material.

Basic Rule

Do something new. If you always do what you've always done, you'll lose your sales participants.

Role Play

Role play is a key activity for engaging sales reps because these are people who interact for a living. They operate by reading situations, establishing relationships, and communicating with customers and corporate staff. Role play gives the sales pro a safe environment to try new things—new ways to approach a prospect, craft a solution to a customer's problem, counter a price or availability objection, explain a product's value, or distinguish herself from her competition. Having a chance to step into a prospect's shoes, take on difficult personality traits or behaviors, voice nagging concerns about a product or service, act as a sales manager coaching a lagging rep, or otherwise assume a role that isn't part of one's typical day opens a very large window through which the trainee can see greater distances. Approaching a topic from both buyer's and seller's positions offers a 360-degree view of the product or service and the full interaction surrounding its sale. And in the classroom setting, mistakes can be made, fears can surface and be assuaged, and confidence can grow.

Role play can be done in a variety of settings. In large groups, only use this technique in a "demonstration scenario"—for example, a sales rep explaining the features and uses of a new product. Choose volunteers who are comfortable being in the spotlight. And make it clear to everyone that role play involves group evaluation and feedback for the "actors" who participate. The feedback will cover what went well and what could have been handled in a better way. It's a form of group coaching, and the actors need to understand it isn't personal criticism.

Role play works best in small groups of four to six people or in triads. These groupings are more intimate opportunities and provide comfortable and safe environments for trainees to practice what they've learned. From the instructor's vantage point, the down side to several small groups is the inability to hear everyone's role play.

Let's consider two formats in greater detail. These two arrangements are good role play starting points for training. Let them serve as foundations on which you build and adapt the role play technique to suit your topics.

Triads

A triad works just the same as a large-group role play, but it splits the participants into groups of three. Limiting the group size relieves some of the anxiety that participants may feel in front of larger audiences. Use this type of role play to help your attendees learn how to overcome objections, practice new listening and questioning techniques, and identify opportunities to close the sale.

Objective: To give participants a safe environment to practice their selling techniques.

Instructions:

▶ Assign one person to play the buyer.

▶ Assign one person to play the salesperson.

▶ Assign one person to act as observer and to give feedback.

▶ Either in writing or verbally, give participants scenarios that outline the situation in which each is playing his or her role. You may choose to give each triad a different scenario, or to give everyone the same situation to enact. Each role you wish your salespeople to play will have specific information that is pertinent to it. Prepare individual "character info" sheets for each role and distribute them to the people taking on those roles. Here's an example: The topic is overcoming objections, and there are three roles: the customer, the sales rep, and the observer. To the "customer," you give an info sheet with this information: "You are stuck on price, and you insist that you can get these widgets cheaper—and with an extended warranty to boot!" To the "sales rep," you give this information: "You know you've got the best widgets (and the best warranty) in the business. But you're not the cheapest. You've got to convince the customer that you and your company offer added value beyond price." And you explain the observer's role this way: "Simply take notes about what you like in the interaction, and where you think there are opportunities for improvement. Keep your feedback supportive—even the negative parts."

▶ Ask the members of the triads to interact as they might in the real world. To make the role play more realistic and meaningful, encourage them to incorporate elements of situations they may have encountered on the job.

▶ Call time and debrief by asking the observers in the triads to offer their feedback. This can be done either in small groups or together in the large group.

▶ Switch roles to expand the experiential learning for everyone. Giving everyone a chance to take two or three roles may mean that you afford less time to each individual role play, but you broaden the perspective exponentially.

You may opt to allow "do-overs" following feedback. Or you may choose to call a time out during the role play so participants can think through or change something. That lets people learn and adjust as they go—a great way to practice and build skills.

The Grinder

Despite its name, the grinder is another low-stress form of role play. Use this to help participants learn

- ▶ new product or service information
- ▶ product or service benefits
- ▶ ways to introduce themselves or the company
- ▶ "canned" sales presentations
- ▶ new questioning techniques
- ▶ active listening techniques
- ▶ tactics for overcoming objections
- ▶ closing techniques.

Objectives: To offer a safe environment for participants to practice what they've learned while they learn from others; to help salespeople identify new ideas.

Instructions:

- ▶ Arrange people in two lines, facing each other. People in one line are buyers; people in the other line are sellers.
- ▶ Give each buyer a product or service she or he is interested in buying from the seller.
- ▶ Start a two-minute role play in which the buyer names the product/service and the seller describes its features and benefits.
- ▶ Call time and ask the buyers to give one minute of feedback to the sellers.
- ▶ Ask the sellers to "grind" to the left (move to the next buyer).
- ▶ Repeat the role play/feedback process at least three more times.
- ▶ Switch the roles of the two lines and distribute products/services to the new buyers. Repeat the whole exercise.

It's important to give each person at least three turns to play the seller. Here's why:

- ▶ The first time, he's getting used to the process.
- ▶ The second time, he's getting real benefit from the feedback.
- ▶ By the third time, he probably has incorporated new ideas and is making improvements in his approach.

Make sure you have the instructions really solid. This is hard for some people to visualize from verbal instructions, so get them in lines, tell them what will happen, and then demonstrate it so they feel more confident at the outset.

The grinder also works well with *really* large groups such as at national sales meetings. It's loud, and it's energizing. Try it—you'll like it!

Review Games

Review games are versatile activities you can use to start your program or check for knowledge at the end of the session. These games can be as high- or low-tech as you'd like. They're great for both large and small groups, and can be led easily in person or in a virtual training environment.

When creating a review game, remember who your audience is. Salespeople are competitive; they love these types of learning opportunities, but things can get out of control if you're not careful. Here are some helpful tips for preparing your games:

- ▶ Research the answers to your questions. If more than one answer might work for any question, include all acceptable answers.
- ▶ Be prepared with solutions to "what-if" scenarios that trainees may pose.
- ▶ Explicitly outline the rules before you begin the game.
- ▶ Update your games often because changes in processes, products, and procedures occur regularly. Don't get caught with outdated information.

If you don't have the technology or software to create electronic games, you'll find these two sample games both versatile and easy to use.

Basic Review Game

Product training is an ideal use for review games. Questions can involve straight product facts, key benefits, or customer problems/scenarios. Keep the information relevant to the topic. Use this kind of game to help participants

- ▶ review materials
- ▶ pretest their level of knowledge and understanding
- ▶ learn about a topic that's dry and boring
- ▶ get motivated at the beginning of the day or after lunch.

Objective: To establish a baseline of participants' knowledge on a topic or to test what they have learned.

Instructions: Break the participants into teams of equal size. Any game that you've played or seen on television can be your model for this activity—*Jeopardy* or *Who Wants to Be a Millionaire?* are obvious choices. Card games or board games like "Trivial Pursuit" or even "Candy Land" will work. As long as you carefully customize your questions to fit the topic you're covering, you can go as low tech as cards or use a commercial game board. You can purchase board games from companies like the Trainer's Warehouse (www.trainerswarehouse.com). If a high-tech approach is more fitting for the group, use PowerPoint to pose the questions or try some of the software packages available at www.training-games.com or www.learningware.com.

One caution in conducting review games: If participants can't answer the questions, they may lose confidence or motivation. Be positive and gentle in handling wrong answers. For example, "Great try, but that's not quite what we're looking for. Does anyone else want to take a shot?" is a great way to commend a trainee for making an effort and to keep him from feeling inadequate in his grasp of the material. Doing reviews with teams rather than individuals increases dialogue and energy and avoids putting individuals on the spot.

Historical Timeline Review Game

Salespeople have to develop their own value proposition to share with potential customers. Part of that value proposition involves the company they represent, so they need to know the company, its history, and its achievements. Use this activity to help participants understand the company history, learn about company successes and milestones, and take away the information they want to incorporate in the value statements they'll share with their customers. This can be an entirely learner-directed process, and it's a welcome alternative to death by PowerPoint for a company history presentation.

Objective: To prompt a discussion of company history in orientations for newly hired sales reps.

Instructions:

▶ Three to four weeks before your training session, send each new employee a summary of the company's history, and ask that she or he read it before coming to the orientation session.

▶ Hang large sheets of poster paper on the training room walls. At the top of each sheet, write one decade in the company's history: 1950s, 1960s, and so forth. (If the orientation is being done online, write the decades on the whiteboard.)

▶ Place a sheet of sticky dots or a roll of tape on each trainee table.

▶ Make an index card deck of historical facts about the company, with no reference to dates. You can include anything that was covered in the summary you sent before the session.

▶ Shuffle the deck and distribute the index cards among all the participants.

▶ Instruct each person to use a sticky-dot to place her card(s) on the correct decade's poster(s).

▶ Give the full group five minutes to look over the arrangement of cards. Let them discuss placements and, as a team, rearrange the cards that are not positioned in the correct decades. The goal is to lay out the company history in the correct order through the decades. Allow 10 minutes for this. Adjust your times accordingly if the class is having a rich discussion or is struggling with the process. Prompt and coach them where needed.

▶ Call time and distribute a summary of the company history, written in paragraph form. Let the group make any corrections to the timeline that are needed. When all the cards are in the right place, ask for volunteers to summarize each decade for the company.

▶ After the game, have everyone share specific information they'll take away and use in forming their value statements.

Case Studies

Case studies are sample situations, either actual scenarios reported by salespeople in the field or stories created to highlight a point or exemplify a technique. These studies offer an opportunity to debate and solve a problem situation your trainees most likely will encounter on the job. You can use these studies to help participants

▶ apply knowledge to a realistic situation

▶ generate informed discussion around an issue

▶ solve problems.

As the trainer, your first step in developing a case is to consider your learning objective. What do you want your learners to understand or be able to do when they've finished working with the study? You need to decide

- ▶ the case study formula—that is, situations that involve the learning you want to convey
- ▶ the specific skills to be taught.

When you have that information, you can follow these steps to create your case study:

1. State the problem.
2. Select a setting that's not an exact replica of the present work environment and the people in it. This will eliminate distractions, avoid unfounded assumptions, and keep everyone on track.
3. Give sufficient background information to help your learners picture the situation.
4. Pose the problem as a question.
5. Prepare clear instructions, explaining what learners need to do with the study details and what questions you want them to answer or discuss.
6. Write facilitator notes, covering the points you're trying to make with this case study.
7. Pilot-test your study with a few people who understand your eventual audience, and revise it as needed. (Don't present it to a live audience without testing it. The test will reveal missing data, confusing language or settings, contradictions, or other flaws that will take the whole activity off track in the classroom.)

As your case study comes together, ask yourself these questions:

1. Is it too detailed? Too general?
2. Is there enough time to present it fully?
3. Is the case too difficult? The more complicated it is, or the more twists you include, the more opportunities you give for it to be argued or misinterpreted.
4. Is the message of the case study easy to understand? Can it be disputed?

5. Is anything in the case distracting? (Does it sound like a company account? Is it too close to your industry? Do any of the players seem familiar? Are any facets of the story locally, socially, or politically controversial enough to get discussions off the point?)
6. Is the dialogue clear?
7. Are your prepared instructions clear and comprehensive?
8. Are your facilitator notes clear and comprehensive?

Editor's Notebook

Using Music in Training

Chris Boyd Brewer's book Music and Learning: Seven Ways to Use Music in the Classroom *(LifeSounds, 1995) is a rich reference about music's influence on learning. Brewer explains that music can*

- *establish a positive learning environment*
- *create an inviting atmosphere*
- *energize people*
- *build anticipation*
- *focus concentration*
- *increase attention*
- *develop rapport*
- *facilitate multisensory learning experiences (by satisfying learners who are more attuned to taking in auditory information—one of the adult learning styles)*
- *release tension*
- *boost memory*
- *provide inspiration and motivation*
- *add fun to the classroom experience.*

Mock Trials and Debates

Trials and debates are great activities because salespeople live and breathe competition. They debate for a living! These activities help them respond to and overcome challenges and objections as they arise.

However, if you have a predetermined outcome in mind, *don't use these methods*. Trials and debates identify and present points from both sides of an issue. The ultimate results—acquittal or conviction in a trial, acceptance or rejection of a hypothesis in a debate—depend on the content and form of the presentation and the final decision of a judge, jury, or audience. If there is a right answer, it is best to just present the right answer.

Mock Trial

This activity can be done in person or in a synchronous online class. If it's happening in a training room, consider arranging the tables and chairs in a layout that resembles a courtroom. Creating a suggestive environment will add to the experience. For each of the witnesses who will be called to testify, prepare an information sheet that describes what facts he or she knows about the case. For each attorney, prepare a detail sheet that states the charge or describes the circumstances under consideration. Give the people in the roles time to prepare (at lunch or brief them the day before).

Objective: To teach participants to think on their feet, overcome objections, and see issues from other perspectives.

Setup:

▶ Ask one volunteer to be the judge—or be the judge yourself.
▶ Assign one volunteer to be the prosecuting attorney. Give him or her the detail sheet.
▶ Assign another volunteer to be the defense attorney. Give him or her the detail sheet.
▶ Assign a witness for the defense who will possess certain knowledge and be cross-examined by the prosecution. Give him or her the prepared information sheet.
▶ Assign a witness for the prosecution who will have certain knowledge (different from that of the defense witness) and be cross-examined by the defense. Give him or her the prepared information sheet.
▶ Ask the rest of the audience to serve as jurors.

Instructions: Give the attorneys a few minutes to speak with their witnesses and find out what those witnesses know about the case.

The judge opens the proceedings very briefly: "We are here today to consider the case of Yummi-O Foods." The trial follows this order of events, with two to three minutes allotted for each one:

1. prosecution's opening remarks
2. defense's opening remarks
3. prosecution's examination of the prosecution witness
4. defense's cross-examination
5. defense's examination of the defense witness
6. prosecution's cross-examination
7. prosecution's closing argument
8. defense's closing argument.

After closing arguments, it's time for the jury to deliberate and deliver a verdict. Give them five minutes. Have the judge poll the jury, asking whether each one finds for the prosecution or for the defense. Whichever decision gets the most votes is the final verdict.

Debriefing: Allow 15 minutes to debrief this activity. Find out from the whole group of jurors what salient points came out, both pro and con. What resonated with each person? What was crucial in their individual decision making?

Debate

Like the mock trial, debate is a very viable option to engage salespeople. The trainer states an hypothesis and two individuals (or teams) present opposing positions on the truth of that hypothesis. Debate is an excellent way to bring out all the aspects of a sales topic, all the benefits and disadvantages of a product or service, or all the strengths of and objections to a sales approach.

Objective: To help participants think on their feet, overcome objections, and see issues from at least one perspective other than their own.

Instructions: Because a debate presents contrasting positions on a debate statement—the hypothesis—prepare one in advance of the training. It should be written as a declarative statement about which two opposing opinions can be argued. For example,

You may want to choose debaters and distribute the hypothesis to them a day or two before class so they have time to prepare their sides of the argument. If that's not feasible, allow at least 30 minutes of class time for debaters to prepare.

In class, follow these steps:

▶ Assign a moderator—or take that role yourself.

▶ If not already done, assign proponents (generally a team, rather than an individual) who will agree with the hypothesis.

▶ Assign opponents (again, a team) who will disagree with the hypothesis.

▶ Ask everyone who is not debating to take notes that they will share as feedback after the debate. If some of your trainees have their laptops with them, suggest that they research points that one or the other side makes.

▶ Ask the moderator to read the hypothesis. (If necessary, give debaters preparation time here. Have some activity ready to fill the observers' time, too.)

▶ Poll the observers to see how many agree with the statement and how many disagree with it. Record the numbers.

▶ Call for remarks in favor of the hypothesis. Allow 10 minutes for these remarks.

▶ Call for remarks opposed to the hypothesis. Allow 10 minutes.

▶ Allow 5 minutes for the opposition to respond to the proponents' remarks.

▶ Allow 5 minutes for the proponents to respond to the opposition's remarks.

▶ Give 5 minutes for the opposition to present a closing statement.

▶ Give 5 minutes for the proponents to present a closing statement.

When the debaters have finished, poll the observers again to learn how many now agree with the hypothesis and how many now disagree. Compare these numbers to the earlier poll. Whichever side has made the most "converts" wins the debate. Ask the observers to share their notes on the two presentations and discuss what helped confirm their views or change their minds.

Improvisation Games

Salespeople improvise every day, on every call. As a sales skill, improvisation's usefulness can't be quantified. It's a technique that's often overlooked in the training setting, but its value there is immense as well. Improv games are some of my favorite exercises, and they prove to be highly effective with salespeople. Because the improvisation skill that is honed in the exercise is directly aligned with the objective of improved selling, the content of the improvisation doesn't have to relate to the topic of the training. This opens lots of fun options for the classroom.

Choose improv activities that support your objectives for the training event. For many exercises, the purposes will be

- ▶ to improve the ability to think on one's feet
- ▶ to practice active, focused listening
- ▶ to develop an acceptance for what other people say, without judging it
- ▶ to generate new and fresh ideas in response to one's surroundings.

In any improvisation exercise, it's a good idea to "neutralize" every participant's official role or title. When all people are perceived to have equal weight in an interaction, everyone's ideas will have equal weight as well.

Brainstorming is a free-form type of improvisation session, and the core principle that we apply in brainstorming should apply in all improv games. Namely, nothing is too impractical or too far out on the fringe. Cognitive weeding out and selective judgments will be made later.

Below, I'll describe two structured improvisation games. For these exercises, the facilitator should demonstrate first, and then participate along with the group. (It's never a good idea to ask learners to do things you're not willing to do.) Because no one should be forced to do an improvisation in front of a group, maintain a safe environment in which people can participate if and to the extent they choose. Letting several games go on simultaneously (sort of bedlam-style) creates enough activity to make the environment safe for everyone.

The Power Think! Improvisation

This game is especially good for helping participants generate fresh marketing ideas—an area where salespeople tend to get stuck on the marketing materials, strategies, and tactics the company provides. At some point in your presentation on marketing, use this game to prompt participants to think differently about how they see a product or service, how they describe or present its features and benefits, or how they identify and define the value they and the company add to the proposed sale.

Instructions:

- ▶ Ask participants to relax for a few moments. Briefly state the topic they'll be power-thinking during this game.

▶ Explain that as words or thoughts come to mind, they should shout them out. Anything that comes up is worth shouting—even if its relationship to the topic isn't immediately apparent.

▶ Ask for a volunteer to write down the thoughts and ideas generated during the activity. Give that person a stack of index cards and explain that one shouted word, phrase, or idea should be written on each card. Keep a stack of index cards for yourself and capture as many of the ideas as you can.

▶ When participants begin to call out their ideas, respond to some of them with "Yes, and . . ." to prompt others to work from those words and ideas, expanding and developing them further.

▶ Allow 10 minutes, and then call time.

▶ Put your cards together with those of your helper, and throw them to the floor in the middle of the room.

▶ Ask for a volunteer to pick up two cards and read the words written there to the whole group.

▶ Ask group members to brainstorm ways they could market and promote their company, product, or service using the ideas or words on those two cards. For example, imagine the words are "ice cream" and "soccer." No matter what the industry, ideas might include hosting an ice cream social, sponsoring the ice cream at a soccer game, volunteering at a soccer field, sponsoring a soccer tournament and serving ice cream there. The list can go on and on.

▶ Several times, repeat the process of picking up and reading two cards and eliciting marketing ideas from the group.

▶ Ask your index-card helper to capture all of the marketing ideas on a flip chart or in an electronic document. After the class, distribute the ideas to all participants to use in whatever ways fit their needs. Remind and encourage them not to be hedged in by typical marketing materials and strategies.

The Sell This! Improvisation

This game—best used in small groups of three to five people—helps participants be more creative in their thinking, listen proactively, work as a team, and respond quickly to challenging or new situations.

Instructions:

▶ Either before the training or with the class, brainstorm a list of fictional product names.

Editor's Notebook

Using Scents in the Training Room

In 2005, the Pakistan Journal of Social Sciences *conducted a study to evaluate the role that our sense of smell plays in cognitive learning. Investigators gave pre- and post-tests to a group of experimental subjects taught in an atmosphere infused with lemon essential oil aromas and to a control group of subjects taught in a normal atmosphere. The results showed that the lemon aroma increased memory and reduced the chance of forgetting valuable information. It also significantly increased participants' attention levels. Perhaps it will prove equally useful in increasing the attention levels of your sales reps, who struggle with the additional distractions of deals in progress, demands from bosses or customers, and opportunities going unheeded while they're in training. Other scents that have been evaluated and proved to produce higher test scores and greater recall and retention in participants are coffee, chocolate, and apple cinnamon.*

There are myriad ways to introduce these helpful scents into your training room. Warmed aromatherapy oils and candles (if open fire isn't against the rules in your training venue); plates of lemon cookies or small boxes of chocolates on the tables; fragrant refreshments such as lemonade, apple cider, hot chocolate, and coffee. Just remember to infuse scents subtly.

▶ Separate the class into small groups, and give one of those product names to each group.

▶ Allow 15 minutes for all groups to come up with the following:

   ▶ a description of the product and what it does

   ▶ a celebrity spokesperson for the product

   ▶ a jingle or a commercial the group can enact.

▶ Have each team present its product to the large group. Here's an example: "Our product is 'Can Can' and it's a new motivational diet drink. Our celebrity spokesperson is Oprah Winfrey. Our jingle will be 'Maybe you couldn't lose weight in the past, but now you Can Can.'"

Other fictional products might be Bling-Bling, Orange Blast, Hidey Ho, Kookie, Cool Colors, Notables, Darl Doodles, Heat Up, Alabaster, Lemon Zestier, Born To, Deluxe Portion, Ganglion, Blue Laze, Lucky Lew, Phony Phylum, Beach Core. Or use terms that are meaningful to your industry. Remember, fictional names should be just that—fictional.

As a trainer, your job here is to help your trainees' acceptance. The point is for groups to work together and support each other's ideas.

■ ■ ■

All of these activity ideas for making your trainings more appealing and engaging for salespeople are only the beginning. There are many resources to help you continue creating meaningful training exercises that not only teach, but also help you motivate your salespeople and help them retain and use what they learn. Try just one activity in your next session. Make it simple and fun, and watch how delighted participants become when they can get up and move.

 Getting It Done

Take the time to identify at least one piece of key content that you can convert into an activity-based training session. Answer the following questions:

1. What is one training module that participants consider dry or that you don't enjoy delivering because of its dull content?
2. Is there an alternative way that this module could be presented?

Identify an activity in this chapter that you can customize to fit one of your training modules. Develop the activity by answering these questions:

1. What is the objective of the activity? What do you want the participants to be able to do?
2. What will the participants learn as a result of the activity?
3. What preparation is necessary on your part?
4. What materials will you need for yourself and for your trainees?
5. What are the individual steps to take in presenting/facilitating the activity?

Phase 5: Evaluating Your Impact

Angela Siegfried

■ ■

What's Inside This Chapter

In this chapter, you'll learn

▶ What to measure when evaluating the training program
▶ How to define success factors
▶ How to calculate return-on-investment.

Your training department contributes directly to the success of the organization. But how do you know for sure? If you can't quantify that impact, then remember that your training department also functions as a cost center, requiring considerable investment by the organization. Senior management wants to know that the investments are yielding results that support organizational objectives, and that's the ultimate business purpose for measuring and evaluating your training programs.

Sales training is a high-stakes endeavor that you are undertaking. And it's all about risk and return. Significant ability to show that an investment in training and learning has produced the right kinds of results will help prompt management to continue allocating funds for your most important initiatives. And the right kinds of results can enhance your status and influence in the organization.

So, how do you get the kind of status and influence you're looking for? First, remember you work in a sales environment, and success in professional selling is measured by the numbers—preferably, the revenue numbers.

Second, surveys and "smile-sheet" evaluations can serve as testimony to the worth of your training department for only so long. It's nice to know that people are enjoying your training sessions, but you need to find out if they're retaining and applying their new knowledge and skills on the job—and if their doing so is helping the company's bottom line.

Third, you need a tangible way to quantify the results of your training programs. Although it can be a daunting task to measure the knowledge and skills of your salesforce before and after a training initiative, and then to calculate the return-on-investment (ROI) that your training produces for the organization, you need to put some substance behind all the work you and your team are doing.

Think About This

Try using ROI metrics for a program that has a future launch date. It's much easier to design metrics and evaluate the ROI for new programs than to do so for programs already in existence.

Remember, your training department not only contributes directly to the success of the organization, it also functions as a cost center, requiring considerable investment by the organization and the training participants. Senior management wants to know that the investments are yielding results that support organizational objectives. That's the ultimate business purpose for measuring and evaluating your training programs.

It's all about risk and return. Significant wins in measuring your training include the ability to show that investment in training and learning has produced the kinds of results that will prompt management to continue allocating funds for your most important programs. Measurement also evinces, maintains, or enhances your status and influence in the organization.

In this chapter, you'll learn what, why, and how to measure what your training participants gain, retain, and apply on the job. And you'll discover how to evaluate the training outcome data in terms that reveal any program's contribution to the organization's objectives.

Preparing to Measure and Evaluate the Results and Impact of Training

Preparation for measuring and evaluating a training program begins when a course is in its development phase. At that time, you should answer the following questions:

- ▶ At what point(s) during and/or following its implementation will the program be evaluated?
- ▶ How will data—such as test results, sales numbers, and performance reviews—be collected?
- ▶ From what sources will data be collected?
- ▶ Who will be responsible for collecting the data?
- ▶ Who will be responsible for analyzing the data?
- ▶ Does this program warrant measuring to such a level?

Consider that last question carefully. I placed it last not because it's unimportant. In fact, most of your training programs will merit attentive measurement and evaluation. But that's not true for every single one of them. For example, is it really necessary to collect extensive data on a one-hour course designed to help sales reps overcome objections? The cost and effort required to provide accurate ROI data can be significant and would not be justified for such a small course. Measuring results and analyzing outcomes takes time and resources. And just as the amount of improvement that a training program yields has to justify the amount of resources invested in creating and implementing the program, the reward realized by measuring results and analyzing their impact has to be equal to or greater than the time and effort dedicated to the measuring and analyzing.

Examples of programs that should be evaluated for business impact are those that

- ▶ link to operational goals and issues
- ▶ are important to strategic objectives

▶ have high visibility

▶ have the attention of top executives

▶ took a significant amount of time to create

▶ have a high development and implementation cost.

Keeping It Meaningful, Measurable, and Simple

Whatever means you choose to measure and analyze training results, make sure not to overcomplicate the process. Doing so can make evaluation frustrating and difficult to execute. Terri O'Halloran, vice president of client development and engagement for the performance improvement company Integrity Solutions, suggests the following three performance measurement basics to help you get started:

1. **Make it meaningful**—Develop a clear link between employee performance and its impact on business outcomes. Begin by asking these questions:

   ▶ What are the key business issues?

   ▶ What's meaningful to senior leadership?

   ▶ What's critical for bottom-line organizational success?

2. **Focus on what's measurable**—For example, how many quotes is a sales agent generating? Of those quotes, how many is she or he closing? This is something that's easy to measure before and after the training, and it ties directly to the organization's goals and bottom line. To identify performance factors that are measurable, ask the following questions:

   ▶ What is your organization already measuring that ties to key business issues?

   ▶ What data currently are being used to manage the business at the executive level?

3. **Keep it simple**—Narrow your focus to just two or three of the metrics that are most meaningful for your senior leadership. Doing so ensures that the scope of work stays manageable and relevant. Depending on the industry your learners are in, these are some metrics you may want to look at:

   ▶ referrals

   ▶ listings

   ▶ employee retention

   ▶ talent recruitment

- sales appointments
- new business relationships
- enhancements to existing business relationships
- sales numbers
- increases in enrollment.

Think About This

The measurement of sales training is a logical, systematic process that addresses the goals, methods, and requirements of data collection and considers how findings will be interpreted, communicated, and achieved. Most important, the measurement of sales training is essential both for assessing the contribution of sales training to business results and for ensuring that the contribution is as robust as it can be. Although each purpose is worthwhile in its own right, together they make sales training measurement a powerful tool for any business.

Be sure that whatever you measure demonstrates how your training achieved the goals set for it. If the goal of your training is to help sales reps increase their close ratios on new accounts, it doesn't make sense to measure how many of the sales reps' existing customers renewed their contracts.

Measuring the Results of Training

Training and performance improvement are all about increasing revenue and decreasing expenses. Historically, however, sales training departments have had few options for measuring the results and business impact of their programs. There are several reasons for this, including a shortage of funds or staff to perform detailed analyses, lack of interest among the leadership team, and difficulty obtaining data from business units after training occurs.

Measuring results—whether in terms of dollars saved, dollars earned, or skills improved—is becoming more important in the current economy. Even if senior management hasn't asked you to prove your value, you need to be able to do just that. Waiting until an executive asks what value you add to the organization before you prepare a cogent and convincing answer is a foolish delay.

Integrating measurement into an already established suite of training courses is tough. It's hard to stop and take stock of the final results of most training efforts because they don't occur in a vacuum. By the time one course or training initiative is nearing completion, most trainers are at least partly involved in planning or designing the next project. So, determining what value training and learning add to business outcomes needs to be planned into every training from the beginning and it needs to be succinct and swiftly accomplished.

Measuring sales training is unique because salespeople have many different goals, all of which should tie to the company's initiatives, strategies, and objectives. Each of those goals offers an opportunity to assess whether performance has improved. Along with a big-picture evaluation of training, the sales function offers many micro areas that can be evaluated. You can measure your sales training effectiveness through the numbers of

- ▶ sales calls made
- ▶ proposals requested and submitted
- ▶ cold calls made
- ▶ cross-sales/up-sales of existing and new products or services
- ▶ closings.

The opportunities to measure a range of results are abundant, and tying those results to previous training isn't difficult; it just takes time.

The Levels of Training Evaluation

Most models for evaluating training are closely related. Their designers build on the work of others and add their own ideas. In 1959, Donald Kirkpatrick introduced the four-level evaluation model, which is widely accepted in training circles. His four

Noted

There are two possible outcomes: If the result confirms the hypothesis, then you've made a measurement. If the result is contrary to the hypothesis, then you've made a discovery.

—Enrico Fermi, nuclear physicist

levels (which will be discussed in greater detail below) are participant reaction and intended action, participant learning, application of learning, and business impact. Later, Jack Phillips built on Kirkpatrick's work by adding a fifth level, a process model, and some guiding principles to ensure standardization and consistency. The combination of Kirkpatrick's and Phillips' work is used on a global basis in a majority of the learning and development functions of many organizations. Here's an explanation of the five levels of evaluation:

1. **Participants' reaction to the training and their planned action(s) as a result of training**—The focus here is on the degree of satisfaction that program participants feel, and how they plan to apply what they've learned.

   This evaluation usually takes the form of a generic end-of-program questionnaire that contains Likert-type scales (0–2, 1–5, and so forth). Typical questions are

   ▶ How effective were the materials?

   ▶ How appropriate was the pace of the course?

   ▶ Was the facilitator effective in explaining the purpose of each activity?

   ▶ Would you recommend this course to others?

   The idea is to get a reaction statement about the class. But don't collect this feedback unless it's going to be used in some meaningful way.

2. **Participants' learning**—This evaluation focuses on the knowledge and/or skills acquired or enhanced during the training program. This evaluation is helpful in determining that the participants have absorbed what has been taught and know how to use it on the job. A common way to assess this is to administer a pre-test and a post-test, with the training intervention occurring between the two tests. The difference in scores will indicate the amount of learning that took place.

   The lengths of the pre- and post-tests should be commensurate with the length of the course. As a rule of thumb, don't ask more than five questions for each hour of content. The longer the program, the fewer the questions per hour. For example, a two-hour program might have 6 questions (3 per hour), whereas a one-week program might have 40 questions (only 1 per hour of content).

3. **On-the-job application of knowledge and skills gained in training**—This level of evaluation focuses on actual application. It determines if the

participants are using their new knowledge on the job. For example, after a training class on how to handle a difficult caller, the participants should be able to demonstrate this skill. A trainee's skill level could be measured in a number of ways: his or her manager could monitor it, a quality control unit could listen to recorded phone calls, or you could stage a difficult call to the trainee as part of follow-up training.

4. **The business impact of participants' new performance as a result of training**—This level of evaluation focuses on results achieved by participants as they successfully apply the program material in their daily work. A participant's manager likely would need to be involved in this phase of evaluation because the manager will be the one measuring that impact. For example, a class on increasing customer retention through improved customer satisfaction would be proved effective if retention numbers increased.

5. **ROI**—The fifth level of evaluation compares the monetary benefits produced by the training program with the program's total costs. Determining ROI requires three calculations—problem cost, program cost, and post-training costs in the problem area. Measuring and evaluating ROI isn't free. It's important to justify the need for tools and resources to start an ROI project.

Think About This

Unlike other training audiences, sales audiences can be thought of as direct contributors to business profitability. Why? Because the people in sales jobs are often asked to be the "face of the business" to current clients and future customers. In that important position, the skills and knowledge contributing to effective selling practice can be directly tied to business success. Furthermore, salespeople are measured on variables such as revenue, customer retention or satisfaction, and account/market penetration. These metrics are bottom-line, business-oriented measurements.

Evaluating the Impact of Training—Getting to the ROI

Essentially, the ROI is a shorthand description of the monetary effect that any sort of initiative produces on an organization's bottom line. Given a situation that is draining revenue from a business, given a quantifiable amount of resources allocated to plugging that drain, and finally given an "after-plug" assessment of the amount of revenues still draining away (if any), it's possible to state that the plugging mechanism returned x dollars for an investment of x dollars and was either successful or not worth that investment.

Remember, salespeople are measured on variables such as revenue, customer retention or satisfaction, account/market penetration, and so on. These metrics are themselves bottom-line, business-oriented measurements. This means that evaluators of sales training don't have to bridge the gap between individual performance and business results, as might be the case with more insulated, nonsales roles like human resources, engineering, or operations. This is a major practical benefit for evaluators.

The impact of training on business results for audiences such as those from product development, the human resource department, logistics, or others may be more indirect and less immediate. In contrast, sales training has an immediate impact on business performance. With sales training, we can use ROI calculations more rapidly and directly to relate learning new behaviors to how those behaviors impact business than in other training areas.

To reach the ROI, four calculations are made. Let's take a closer look at those calculations, and place them in a sample scenario.

The First Calculation: What Does the Problem Cost?

To begin, you need a baseline description of the problem to be addressed by some (hopefully corrective) investment—for our purposes, sales training. This first figure defines the existing situation. It's the core business issue that is prompting the training investment and against which the post-training situation will be evaluated.

Let's consider a sample scenario to describe a problem in terms of performance figures and at-risk revenue. This example illustrates potential annual income at risk for a call center. The call center's problem is in the number of calls that are dropped by operators every day. (We'll return to this scenario two more times to show how we use the baseline financial description of the problem in our quest to discover the ROI.)

The sample scenario: The call center has 200 customer calls per day. Five percent of all incoming calls are dropped by the people answering them. The company has determined that the average completed sale is worth $500. With these figures, the company can identify the amount of money that is being lost in dropped calls each day, week, and year:

200 calls x 5% dropped x $500 income per average call = $5,000 lost each day.

In a five-day week, that's $25,000. And over the course of a year, the company is putting at risk a total of $1,300,000. That's the first figure we'll use in discovering the ROI.

The Second Calculation: How Much Is Being Invested in Training?

Training costs include anything necessary to conduct a training. As a sales instructor, it's easy for you to ignore the costs of every aspect of your training—leaving that to management or the accounting department. But your keen eye is needed to assess all training expenses. You must account for all the costs, including the candy on your table, your salary and that of other instructors, the paper your materials are printed on, and lots more.

Good budgeting will help you accomplish this. Create a spreadsheet to track all of your expenditures for every training you deliver. Be diligent in logging every item, no matter how small. You may not have access to some of the most sensitive costs (such as salary), so reasonable estimates will suffice.

Now let's return to our call center scenario. Senior management wants to reduce the daily number of dropped calls from 5 percent to 1 percent, and the training department's help has been requested. Your sales training team develops training around new customer service practices and techniques on call transfer processes. The cost to develop and deliver this program is $50,000.

The Third Calculation: How Much Does the Problem Cost After Training?

The last calculation needed before ROI can be determined requires a post-training assessment of the situation in the original problem area. Being sure to compare apples with apples, the problem area is evaluated again to see what is happening there.

Back to our call center. Sixty to 90 days after the training solution is implemented, the call volume remains the same—200 calls come into the center each day. And the company's estimated per-call value is still $500. But now the operators are dropping only 1 percent of the calls that come in. We return to our first-calculation formula to determine the "new normal" in the call center:

200 calls x 1% dropped x $500 income per average call = $1,000 lost each day.

In a five-day week, that totals $5,000, and over the course of one year, it results in a revenue loss of $260,000. We now subtract that revenue loss from the revenue loss calculated at the outset to arrive at the program benefit:

$$\$1,300,000 - \$260,000 = \$1,040,000.$$

The Final Calculation: ROI

Calculating ROI makes the ultimate business case for (or perhaps against) a training program. In the financial world, ROI is a measurement of historical data, including the ratio of the money lost in or gained from an endeavor to the money invested in that endeavor. In the world of sales training, it's no different. ROI is the monetary value of business performance compared with the cost of the program.

Here's the two-step formula for calculating ROI:

Net program benefits = Gross program benefits – Program costs.
ROI = Net program benefits ÷ Program costs x 100.

Multiplying by 100 will enable you to show your ROI as a percentage—and easily understood metric. This is the same formula used in evaluating other investments where ROI traditionally is reported as earnings divided by investment.

So let's go back a final time to our call center scenario. We have found that our training has produced an annual increase of $1,040,000 in revenue by reducing the number of dropped calls to 1 percent. And we know that the company invested $50,000 in our training program. Now let's figure the ROI:

$1,040,000 benefit – $50,000 cost = $990,000 net benefit.
$990,000 ÷ $50,000 x 100 = 1,980% ROI.

This type of ROI is important because the salesforce is the face of the business to customers, and the skills and knowledge that contribute to effective selling directly impact business success. The numbers calculated above are also likely to lead to a favorable impression of the training initiative by key stakeholders—and those stakeholders will be more likely to continue down the path you've charted for them.

Calculating the Intangibles

It is equally important to measure the intangible benefits that a training course provides. Some training benefits can't be credibly converted to money, but you should report these benefits because they are part of the business case for training. In their book *Make Training Evaluation Work* (ASTD, 2004), Jack Phillips, Patti Phillips, and Toni Hodges offered these examples of intangible benefits:

▶ increased job satisfaction
▶ employees' increased commitment to the organization
▶ enhanced teamwork
▶ improved customer service
▶ fewer complaints
▶ less conflict.

ROI calculations can be varied. And the calculation must meet the needs of the sales team. So where should you start? The answer is found in taking a blended approach.

Editor's Notebook

A colleague and I were talking about ROI calculation. She made a great point in helping me understand that the ROI calculation (how you measure success) must be based on a proper needs assessment (what you measure). She shared a story to drive home the point: Her preliminary data and interviews with her prior sales management team suggested that dramatic improvements to her sales team's onboarding process were needed. Potential sales in global emerging markets were being lost because the corporation was unable to attract and ramp up new hires skilled in sales. The senior vice president in her company articulated this need succinctly: "We need an onboarding program that not only recruits, but up-skills and then helps retain the sales talent essential for an effective, enduring sales organization."

Stakeholders and needs assessment data agreed that, in terms of goals, such a program would have to quickly attract, engage, integrate, and equip new hires in sales to respond to emerging opportunities. From there, the ROI data could be gathered and the calculations could be made.

Her story came to a great ending. She developed a new-hire sales training to achieve the goals. Measurements put in place were based on a set of mutually reinforcing onboarding components for developing new-hire knowledge, building robust global and local sales practice communities, and providing the mentoring essential for sales effectiveness. The ROI was positive and results were achieved. It was a win for her, a win for the senior vice president, a win for the sales team, and ultimately a win for the customers. And it all started with a proper needs analysis.

The moral of the story? Build your ROI calculation process into the very beginning—starting with the needs analysis.

Qualitative vs. Quantitative: The Importance of a Blended Approach

Evaluating the effectiveness and business impact of sales training should be rigorous, but also practical. Many tools are available for measuring sales training, and each has its own strength and weakness (see table 8-1). For that reason, evaluating a sales training program should use a blended approach that enables evaluators to capitalize on each tool's strength and benefit while avoiding its inherent weakness and shortcoming.

■ ■ ■

Invest in your training evaluation, measure it, test it, measure it again. You are sure to make an impact the first time you present the results to your senior leadership. That in turn builds credibility and proves how important the educational investment is.

Getting It Done

To determine what levels of evaluation to use for specific training programs, ask yourself the following questions:

1. *How will the evaluation results be used?* If you're pilot-testing a new program, for example, the level-one (participant reaction) evaluation will be very helpful, especially if you let participants know that their feedback will be used to modify this and future programs. When there is no possibility that the content can be updated before it is presented, don't ask about the content's appropriateness.

2. *What has the sponsor of the training requested as proof of learning?* If the sponsor wants to see how the training is affecting results, but not necessarily in terms of dollars, a level-four (business impact) evaluation is appropriate. But if the sponsor simply needs to see that learning occurred, a pre- and post-test evaluation will suffice.

3. *Is the training mandatory?* If so, there really is no need to do an ROI study because the return doesn't matter. A level-one evaluation may be sufficient.

4. *Will you have access to the data you need to do higher-level analyses?*

Table 8-1. Selecting the Right Evaluation Tool: A Blended Approach

Tool	Benefits/Strengths	Costs/Weaknesses	Examples of Good Use
Qualitative tools			
Observation	Direct experience of a sales training workshop or demonstration of a learned behavior on the job	Costly to cover all instances of training or on-the-job expression of desired behaviors	Assessing training at pilot and early launch stages Selectively assessing behavioral on-the-job changes resulting from training
Interview	Insights into what others (such as participants and their managers) experienced and what they think about it	Time consuming to schedule and conduct interviews; data is the subjective perspectives of a limited number of interviewees	Exploring the training and post-training experiences of participant and stakeholder samples
Focus group	A sample of common and shared vs. individual experiences	Less vocal individuals may not be willing to share impressions openly	Debriefing training events at pilot or later implementation stages through selective sampling
Quantitative tools			
Survey	Broad, understandable data for comparing the experiences of all or large samples of participants	Not necessarily the reasons why participants think the way they do	As a basis for assessing the strength or representation of insights gained through interviews
Metrics tracking	Objective data that demonstrates the bottom-line impact of training (for example, quota attainment, customer satisfaction)	To be credible, must be linked to training through a business value chain	As evidence of training's business impact and of the need for more rigor; using a control group is recommended

9

Making Your Sales Training Stick with Coaching

Tim Ohai

What's Inside This Chapter

In this chapter, you'll learn

▶ What sales coaching is
▶ How to make your sales training stick through coaching
▶ How to help managers become great coaches
▶ Strategies for sales coaching
▶ When coaching isn't appropriate.

An important aspect of great sales training is the ability to make a lasting impact. To do so, you must build a follow-up program into your overall sales training and development plan. Let's face it: Designing and delivering great sales training that hits the mark with the sales teams is definitely important, but you'll find that much of the value is derived out in the field and after the class is over. That's why you need a follow-up plan to make your sales training stick.

Basic Rule

To continue realizing the value of sales training, help sales managers and salespeople align with the same approach taught in the training session. To accomplish this goal, integrate sales coaching with your sales training outcomes. Done correctly, sales coaching will enable your sales managers to focus product knowledge, industry knowledge, selling skills, and company-specific requirements into teachable moments right when they matter.

There are three ways to achieve a high degree of focus in your sales coaching efforts. First, all sales managers should participate in a management version of the sales training you're delivering. This will help ensure a common language and understanding of the knowledge and skills expected. Second, managers should also receive sales coaching training to ensure role modeling and an approach focused on observing others, offering developmental feedback, and providing the right amount of motivation. Third, managers must realize their role in reinforcing the skills and actions taught in the training. Managers can undo sales training with just a few words, and that could create inefficiency and missed opportunities at the point of sales.

How Coaching Can Help

Professional selling is a high-skill and intense job. Helping your sales team attain peak performance requires an integrated approach to processes, tools, and technology. Although many organizations focus on these critical aspects of sales performance, they often overlook the most important factor of all, their people. Effective sales coaching puts the people dynamic in its proper place—front and center. Teaching your sales management team how to hold effective sales coaching conversations can help them realize the company go-to-market strategy for you and your team. Sales coaching techniques can help your sales leadership focus on the right activities that get results. If you want to help your sales team sell consistently and increase revenue quarter after quarter, you have to help them adjust and refine as they continue to improve. Doing so will help them engage clients throughout the entire sales process and keep up with the buyer decision-making process.

Sales Coaching Defined

Using sales coaching as a follow-up to any sales training program involves making sure that the salesperson's best performance is linked to sales results. To link the individual's performance to sales results, you must understand two major elements.

Noted

Sales coaching is minute-by-minute sales leadership; it's grassroots sales leadership.

—Linda Richardson, founder and chair of Richardson, Inc.

First, the sales rep's own internal potential (his or her personal best) determines the focus of the coaching. You can't set reasonable goals that are beyond a person's limits, no matter how hard you try. By focusing on the inner potential of the individual, the sales coach has the best chance of converting the desired result into reality.

Second, coaching is very much about drawing out, not putting in. In other words, the focus of what a salesperson can do best is determined by the salesperson. She or he may not know what strengths exist in the beginning, but the effective coach will uncover those over time. By placing the emphasis on drawing out those strengths, the sales rep more readily accepts responsibility for using his or her strengths, even when the coach isn't there.

Coaching is about getting the best out of any "player." So what's the biggest obstacle to that process? It's people who are in the role of coach, but really are just super players themselves. Have you ever seen a sales coach who always takes over the call when the sale gets bogged down (no matter how small the deal)? This is the same sales coach who complains the loudest about not having enough time to do other aspects of the job. Maybe it's because this coach hasn't built the capabilities of his players to take more responsibility for their own performance.

Helping Managers Become Great Coaches

In the realm of coaching, many skills come into play. Communication skills, managing interpersonal dynamics, critical thinking skills, and time management are a few of them. Instead of creating a long list of essential skills and abilities, help your sales managers concentrate on three very important concepts. Like anchor points that keep a boat from drifting away, these concepts will enable your sales managers (or any sales coaches) to keep their focus on bringing the best out of their sales reps' own abilities, instead of trying to push their own knowledge and abilities into their reps.

The three anchor points of sales coaching that you want sales managers to display are

▶ observation
▶ motivation
▶ developmental feedback.

Lacking any one of these aspects will negate the effectiveness of the coaching (see figure 9-1). Observation and motivation without feedback constitutes cheerleading. Offering motivation and feedback without observation is like trying to coach players when you've never seen them play. And observation and feedback without motivation is pointless.

Figure 9-1. Anchor Points of Successful Sales Coaching

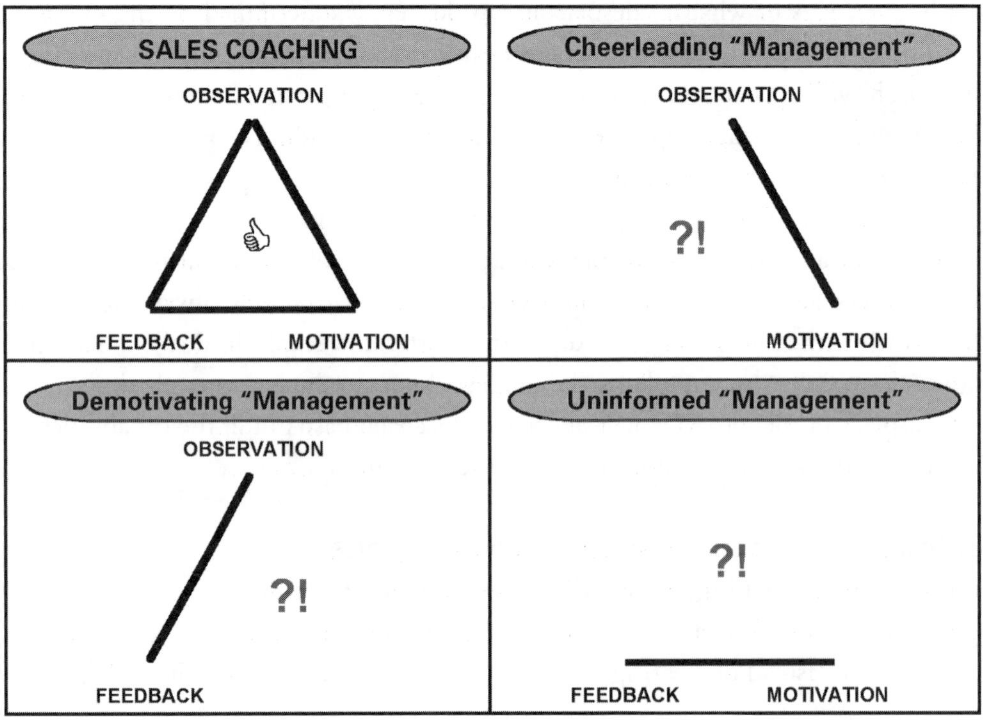

By building the anchor points as the foundation of any sales coaching experience, your sales managers will keep the often overwhelming desire to "make plans" in check with developing great players while resisting the urge to be great players themselves.

Observation

Perhaps the most commonly ignored aspect of observation is the fact that the mouth is closed. Sales coaching demands that your sales managers build observation into their game plans. Whether it be simply shadowing a salesperson as she or he goes through the day or going into specific situations that the rep needs to focus on, the sales manager should make sure that there are enough opportunities to see the difference between patterns and anomalies. Too often, the sales manager sees the misstep of one moment, then proceeds to work on helping the sales team member improve in that one area. If the purpose is to increase sales or make plans, put the energy of sales coaching into the areas that have the biggest impact.

How well do you measure the observations that go with sales coaching? If you're not measuring observation, how do you know it's being done? Here are some ways to measure the first anchor point, observation:

▶ Count the number of times a sales manager goes out to observe her or his salespeople. How often are they getting away from their desks?

▶ Count the number of coaching reports completed at the end of the observation. Are managers recording their observations to review later?

▶ Assess the quality of the coaching reports. When you look at the reports, do you find they have enough substance?

▶ Collect feedback from the sales reps. Do employee surveys, interviews, and so forth indicate that the manager is actually observing in silence?

Motivation

Motivation comes in a variety of forms. To be sure, "show me the money" has become a fairly common focus for motivating sales professionals. But just getting a bonus check will bore even the best of salespeople eventually.

Internal motivations often deal with personal values and drives. These motivations may be

▶ what the salesperson has learned is associated with success

▶ the level of confidence that the sales rep possesses

▶ how the salesperson is "wired."

Think About This

Successful sales managers know what internal and external motivations elicit the desired responses from their salespeople. And the motivations are different for each person.

The key here is to help your sales manager identify these internal motivations, assess how strong they are, and keep the sales team members focused on activities that help them experience those motivational triggers in a positive way.

External motivations often deal with environmental factors over which the sales-person may or may not have influence. Examples include

- ▶ the sales bonus system
- ▶ extra responsibilities or special assignments
- ▶ promotions
- ▶ improvements in internal processes.

To be a great sales trainer, you need to focus on creating an environment where both the sales team and the sales manager can satisfy their internal motivations. More important, the environment must enable the sales team members to push farther and harder to achieve their best, especially when they have the support of your sales management team.

How well do you measure the motivation that goes with sales coaching? Again, if you're not measuring it, how do you know it's being done? Here are some ways to measure the second anchor point, motivation:

- ▶ Count the number of times a coach uses contests and local rewards. Are salespeople being rewarded for extra effort?
- ▶ Monitor the visibility of individual sales results on the team. Who is in first place, and so on?
- ▶ Assess the quality of the coach's insights into the members of the sales team. Does the manager talk about what motivates the team members and why?
- ▶ Collect feedback from the sales reps. Do employee surveys, interviews, and the like indicate that the coach is actually leveraging internal and external motivation?

Developmental Feedback

Perhaps the most important (and most difficult) aspect of sales coaching is providing the feedback. Not only must your sales management team deliver feedback in ways that the sales team will actually listen to, it also must not take away from the motivation that has been (or is being) established. Unfortunately, feedback is often delivered as a dose of simple error correction. Although error correction has a place in the discussion, if all the sales reps hear are the mistakes they make, eventually they'll tune out the message and the messenger. The key is to make feedback exactly what it's intended to be: observations and critique designed to help someone grow. A simple, but highly effective, method you can teach your sales managers is the Keep/Stop/Start method (figure 9-2):

Figure 9-2. The Keep/Stop/Start Feedback Method

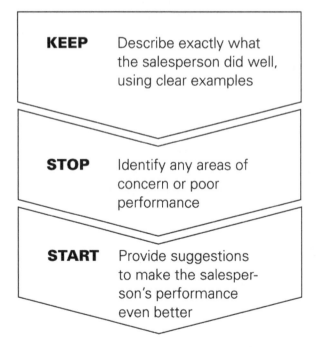

KEEP — Describe exactly what the salesperson did well, using clear examples

STOP — Identify any areas of concern or poor performance

START — Provide suggestions to make the salesperson's performance even better

▶ **Begin with the Keep**—Have the sales manager describe exactly what the salesperson did well, using clear examples.

▶ **Move to the Stop**—Have the sales manager identify any areas of concern or poor performance.

▶ **Finish with the Start**—Have the manager make constructive suggestions about what the individual can do to make his or her performance even better.

Basic Rule

The sales manager does not have to be the expert. With the right coaching, some players actually become better than the coach ever was.

The beauty of this method is that the coaching conversation provides space for the sales manager to bring in both observation and motivation. Also, suggest that the sales manager turn the Keep/Stop/Start model into a questioning process. By asking the salesperson to answer the questions first, three things happen:

▶ First, the sales rep learns how to evaluate her own performance (whether or not the coach is present).

▶ Second, the sales rep can show that she is aware of her own mistakes, so that the coach doesn't need to hammer on a point that's already understood.

▶ Third, the sales rep actually may identify things that the coach didn't see. This is especially important when one is trying to draw out the salesperson's best (not what the coach thinks "the best" should look like).

Editor's Notebook

Feedback should be treated like food. First, keep it fresh. If a sales manager can't give feedback in a reasonable amount of time, don't give it at all. ("Reasonable" in this case is directly correlated with the length of time you might keep leftovers in the fridge before throwing them out.) If the issue is a big deal and the manager didn't give the player feedback promptly, there will be another opportunity soon enough. Second, control the portion size. Keep feedback in digestible portions that don't overwhelm the salesperson. This means two or three points of feedback at any one time.

How well do you measure the developmental feedback that goes with sales coaching? Here are some ways to measure the third anchor point, developmental feedback:

▶ Consider the topics covered in the coaching reports. When you look at the reports, do you find they include developmental topics?

▶ Monitor the use of developmental progress reports as a part of the coaching toolkit. Is there a record of progress for the salesperson?

▶ Assess the progress made developmentally. How often is the same gap being mentioned as an "opportunity for improvement?"

▶ Collect feedback from the salespeople being coached. Do employee surveys, interviews, and so forth indicate that coaches are consistently providing developmental feedback to improve individual performance?

Sales Coaching Strategies

So how does one start to turn all of these elements into a sustainable development plan? What does one do with those who can (but won't), those who can't (but want to), and those who can (and will)? You can help your sales management team develop sound coaching strategies by understanding the difference between the salesperson's skill and the salesperson's will.

Notice how the grid in tool 9-1 is divided into three zones: Crisis, Command, and Develop. This grid helps you determine who on your sales staff needs immediate coaching attention. Staff members in the Crisis zone have low skill and low will (motivation). Staff members in the Develop zone have moderate skill and moderate motivation. Sales team members in the Command zone are top performers; they have high levels of skill and are highly motivated.

The Crisis zone should be the manager's first priority. Chances are good that sales team members in this zone are taking up the most coaching time by continually generating problems that need to be addressed by managers. The interesting thing to note is that the salespeople in Crisis didn't start that way. Somehow, they drifted into this zone, and it's the responsibility of the sales manager to address this drift immediately. Sales team members should be coached out of the Crisis zone (or off the sales team) within six months. This may sound aggressive, but unless the salesperson readily feels the pressure, the manager will never have the time to invest in other team members.

Tool 9-1. The Skill–Will Grid

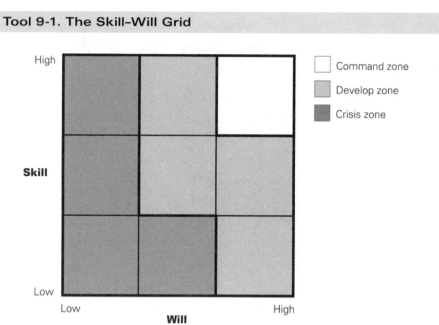

The manager's second priority is to focus on the Command zone. If this focus seems counterintuitive when one looks at the (potentially many) other opportunities on the team, it should be noted that people who are leveraged from the position of their strengths have the capacity to generate the highest level of results. Although there are rare examples of maximum sales outputs already being generated, the top performers typically can make a greater impact on overall sales performance than can the average performers combined.

Another benefit of the sales coach focusing on the Command zone is the spread of coaching responsibility to areas where the quick and effective impact can be made. In other words, don't let your managers limit the coaching given to sales reps in the Command zone to just increasing their already high skill and high will. Rather, have the management team give them the extra responsibility to reach out and coach someone else to increase skill or will (focusing on only one dynamic at a time). This outreach will give the manager a chance to see if these sales reps can coach (identifying those who should be groomed to manage teams of their own) and it will give the manager time to coach the sales team members in the Develop zone (who have more complex developmental needs). Remind the manager to include this extra coaching responsibility in the Command salesperson's development plan.

One further piece of guidance: If your management team is creating a coaching plan for an individual who has more than one need in the Crisis zone, the team should prioritize on the basis of the buying/selling process. For example, if the person in the Crisis zone is weak in both initial needs analysis and deal closing, the manager should focus first on the competencies related to initial needs analysis (because it is the earlier phase in the buying/selling process). Typically, by helping the manager coach a salesperson to improve performance in the earlier steps of the process, the latter steps improve as part of a domino effect. Using the example given, the strengths of the insights discovered at the beginning of the engagement become strengths in the negotiations to close the deal.

By using this approach to priority zone development planning, the successful sales manager is able to accomplish two things:

1. The manager can create development plans linked to the appropriate need (skill versus will) that go beyond the overused elements of "take a leadership course" or "improve your computer skills" that eventually find their way to the annual development plan. The increase in both legitimacy and usefulness will create energy in the sales team members and enhance their willingness to be developed.

2. This process will improve overall team performance within six months, creating time to enjoy a new level of performance, increased confidence, and increased trust that the coaching generated.

When Coaching Is Not Appropriate

One of the most important discussions you can have with your sales management team centers on helping members know when *not* to coach. Unfortunately, coaching is often used as a salve for every situation. Such overuse undermines the enormous value that sales coaching can have in generating revenue.

The first indicator that sales coaching is not appropriate is when the salesperson isn't coachable. There's no point trying to help someone who is unwilling to be observed, to be motivated, and to receive feedback. The caution in this situation is to evaluate the coach first. If the coach has a prior history with the sales rep that undermines credibility or trust, the rep usually will resist being coached until that prior history is resolved. In these cases, a third party may need to be brought in to assess whether the rep is coachable. Again, for emphasis, coachability is defined by the degree in which someone is willing to be observed, to be motivated, and to receive feedback.

The second indicator that sales coaching is not appropriate is the organization not supporting it. This lack of support may be blatant or veiled. A blatant lack of support would look like leaders who devalue sales coaching verbally or say that it isn't a priority. A veiled lack of support occurs in an organization where sales coaching is touted as important but is drowned out in a deluge of competing priorities (such as administrative overload, attendance at too many noncustomer events, and an excessive emphasis on getting end results). Sadly, a veiled lack of support is the most common obstacle to sales coaching.

If the need is not about bringing out an undeveloped ability, it's a third indicator that sales coaching isn't appropriate. If the goal of coaching is to bring out the salesperson's best, don't use sales coaching when the need is to put "the best in." If the sales team member doesn't have any innate ability to sell, no amount of sales coaching will transform him or her into a high-performing sales professional.

Think About This

Sales competence frameworks, remuneration strategies, and training programs all have tremendous value, but they rest on the strength of sales coaching. If the coaching is in place and active, those other initiatives can be leveraged to increase an organization's selling capacity. If not, the initiatives will quickly fade into background noise as salespeople focus on other things, like making plans.

Finally, all good intentions aside, customer calls can go horribly wrong, even with the coach present. To avoid genuine business damage, plan for these moments in advance. Before going to talk to a customer, decide how the call will be handled if the salesperson stumbles. Here are some guidelines to help you do that:

▶ If going to see a top-tier customer or prospect, the stakes are probably higher. The coach may need to switch roles and become a salesperson.
▶ If going to see a customer or prospect who is not part of the top tier, the stakes are much lower. The coach should refrain from becoming a sales rep.

These situations provide the best opportunity to see what areas need to be developed in the salesperson.

■ ■ ■

Any organization that is involved in the selling relationship understands how important its sales system is. And although it is commonly recognized that the selling profession now is seeing a massive shift in salesforce demographics, many organizations are seeking to standardize key elements of their sales systems to increase and accelerate performance. The key to these initiatives is to understand the absolute necessity of sales coaching as a core enabler.

Getting It Done

Using tool 9-1, take a few minutes to assess your sales team members. Place each person's initials in the box that best describes their standing in your sales organization. Then answer the following questions:

1. What key actions will you take within the next two weeks for those sales team members in the Crisis zone?
2. What key actions will you take within the next two weeks for those in the Command zone?
3. What key actions will you take within the next two weeks for those in the Develop zone?

10

Leveraging Subject Matter Experts for Impact

Angela Siegfried

■ ■

What's Inside This Chapter

In this chapter, you'll learn

▶ The value of working with subject matter experts to enhance your training

▶ How to engage and collaborate with subject matter experts

▶ Ways to coach nontrainer experts to develop their skills as content designers and presenters.

As a sales training professional, you're probably an expert in some aspect of your sales training content, but you can't be expected to know everything. That's why subject matter experts (SMEs) are so important in creating a comprehensive and successful training program. An SME can be your content lifeline when you need training help that only a true expert can provide. In addition to its unique rewards, however, collaborating with an SME presents its own set of challenges that you must be ready to handle. This chapter will help you find the right SME with the knowledge and skills you need, and it will show you how to prepare any SME to add value to the training program you're designing for your salesforce.

Editor's Notebook

My own learning and performance background is in leadership development, and my sales experience was in aviation. When I entered the financial services field, I knew consultative selling practices and had good delivery skills, but I had no expertise in systems, products, or guidelines. I needed help from the experts who handled contracts and knew our products, pricing, guidelines, and technology inside and out. I needed them to design and help deliver training. Reaching out to the SMEs turned out to be the best decision for our training organization. Over time, it has helped our team establish solid relationships, produce relevant and useful content, and open opportunities for each of the experts' departments to convey critical information to the salesforce.

Think About This

Nearly all salespeople and instructors (more than 90 percent) define sales training to include sales skills training. At the same time, 31–55 percent of salespeople and instructors don't include product training, industry training, or technical training in that definition.

Why Collaborate with an SME?

For sales professionals, sitting through a class that doesn't engage them is a brutal experience, especially if it's clear that the instructor or facilitator is winging the content. As a sales trainer, you have a commitment to your participants and your company to ensure that the sales team is prepared and enthusiastic about representing the product or service your company is offering in the marketplace—and that means you must present top-quality knowledge-sharing and skill-building experiences for the sales staff. That's a big responsibility to carry alone, so get over any reluctance to use an SME. You will find that an SME may be a partner who saves a sales training program. Here are just a few of the advantages an SME offers:

▶ **Saves time**—On average, it takes 20 hours to design 1 hour of content. You can reduce this time significantly by working with SMEs. Remember, they hold the key to the knowledge door. They've heard the questions before, found the answers, and know the topic. Why not go to a reliable source for content research and development?

Think About This

The success of a training program isn't entirely dependent on the content. Sales training may fail simply because the person leading the learning doesn't make a good impression. It's imperative that every person who delivers a portion of the training—experienced instructor or subject matter expert—builds rapport, gains participants' trust, and finds opportunities to encourage respect for one another and for the talents each person brings to the classroom.

▶ **Creates a more engaging delivery system**—No one wants to sit in a classroom for two weeks with a single instructor, not even a dynamic one. Variety helps motivate and engage your salespeople to participate fully in the learning. Offering sessions taught by several people makes a course more interesting, and ensures that more robust content is offered. Because people respond differently to different personality and presentation styles, having more than one presenter offers more opportunities to reach all the participants.

▶ **Enhances credibility**—Salespeople want to hear your training content from people who actually possess the knowledge and skills being conveyed, people who live and breathe the content every day. If the information is being shared by a bona fide expert, participants know when they ask the questions to which they really need answers, the information they get is accurate and current. Putting SMEs in front of your class of salespeople prompts participants' buy-in for the content and the presenter and lends credibility to the overall sales training program.

▶ **Builds relationships**—Bringing an SME into the design and delivery of your sales training program can build lasting relationships in a couple of ways. When you reach out to departments and people outside your training team, you acknowledge their worth and expertise, and you begin to build friendships. Although at the outset the SME is helping you, the relationship generally becomes reciprocal at some point because you'll find at least one opportunity to offer something that can help the SME and her team. Relationships also are kindled between salespeople and SMEs. Sales reps working in the field usually don't spend time in the office. Putting your SMEs in the room with the sales reps offers tremendous networking opportunities as the sales reps meet inside people who can help them when they return to the field.

Think About This

The greatest disservice you will do to your stakeholders and yourself is to design content without consulting or engaging the people who know the topic inside and out.

Working with SMEs

You will find that collaborating with SMEs is easy. Before beginning any conversation with SMEs you may want to bring into your course, it's important that you truly understand the needs and expectations of your learners and your organization. Only when you've completed a thorough needs analysis do you start fleshing out the details of the training program.

Start the course design process by developing a topic outline and prioritizing the planned content within it. It's likely that you immediately will discover areas of knowledge or skill that should be developed and perhaps taught by people with daily working experience. Discover which departments in the organization deal with those subject areas, and then identify the leaders in each of those departments. Reach out to the leaders and ask them to suggest individuals who might help with the design and delivery of your planned content. Because the skills to design and the skills to deliver are very different, you may want to work with two or more SMEs. You'll know this by assessing each person's individual background to look for specific design or delivery experience. You can also find out the level of expertise by understanding each individual's level of education (that is, industry certifications, certificates, classes taken, and so forth). You can also ask each expert relevant questions to discover how much she or he knows about design, delivery, or both.

Think About This

Leaders often are looking for opportunities to help develop their employees. When you are able to present the opportunity to design or deliver content as a professional development activity, you may be helping fill a departmental need that the leader has identified. This is a chance to give back in exchange for the leader's and the expert's help in your courses.

When you have defined the training needs that are prompting you to prepare a course, have chosen the content for which you need or want expert contributions, and have identified the person or people you'd like to engage to develop or present that material, you should follow a structured process that both explains to the SMEs what you expect and coaches them for success in collaborating with you and in training members of the sales team.

When an SME has been recommended to you, contact that person directly and ask if he or she is available and interested in participating in the training design and/or delivery. Briefly explain your expectations and the specifics of the intended training. Be prepared to estimate and justify the time requirement by describing the business need so you can counter objections to the request. Ensure that the SME understands and agrees to the project commitments at the outset.

When your SME has agreed to participate, prepare them for what the task entails. Meet with your expert and follow these steps:

1. Share results from your needs assessment/analysis.
2. Explain the key content areas you wish to include in the training.
3. If you have not already been explicit about this, describe the kind of contribution you're seeking—content research, course design help, knowledge/skills delivery, or a combination of them.
4. Discuss objectives and outcome expectations for the course overall and for the SME's specific contributions.
5. Take time to answer questions and allay any concerns that the SME expresses.
6. Set a date to meet again and ask the SME to bring to that meeting the ideas for content they wish to include, based on the objectives you've explained.

As you work with the SMEs, you may discover that you need to spend more time clarifying needs and objectives so that they bring the most useful material to the course. If your SMEs don't understand the big-picture purpose for the training you've asked them to participate in or if they don't know what the learners should be able to do after they leave the class, their contributions aren't likely to meet the participants' needs. Take time to educate your SMEs on the importance of having firm learning objectives with which to align the content presented in training, and explain the specific objectives of the training in which you've asked them to help. As a guide to those specific objectives, you can use the information you gathered from the second phase of the Rapid Development Blueprint (chapter 4) to help you create great learning objectives. Be very clear in explaining the results you and the company hope to see from the SMEs' contributions.

In the training room, an SME will have a limited amount of time to connect with and engage your course participants, so give him as much information as you can during the course design phase. Make sure each SME has all of these:

▶ the class agenda, with appropriate time guidelines for his portion of the work
▶ objectives for each module of the course
▶ background information about the people who will attend the course—for example, their tenure with the organization, career/job experience, department hot topics
▶ information about any individual challenges the SME is likely to encounter in the classroom and tips for addressing them.

Coach Your SMEs for Success in Training

Your role as a professional sales instructor includes coaching and mentoring. You're a leader, but your success depends on the knowledge, skills, and ability of someone other than you or your team members. Although your primary responsibility may be to deliver content, you also must develop SMEs who can partner successfully with you and your training team.

Coaching is so important that chapter 9 covered it in detail. Just as in sales coaching, you'll have to work with your SMEs to provide the proper observation, motivation, and feedback so they can improve continually.

When it comes to coaching your SMEs, help them realize and learn that what they know is different than *teaching* what they know. People with high skill levels often can't articulate how or why they do something; they just do it. When people get into a groove where they're comfortable with a body of knowledge or a skill, they sometimes forget that others don't have the same basic understandings. That makes it difficult for them to teach what they know and what they do. If you expect incredible content and stellar presentation skills from your SMEs, you have to coach it out of them.

Coaching your SME begins at the very first encounter with the expert and continues through the entire relationship you share. Coaching can take many forms, and you should base your choice of form on the SME's learning style and your physical proximity to the SME. If you're fortunate enough to have face-to-face meetings, you can get together regularly and simply discuss progress on the content and the positive and constructive elements of the planned delivery.

Prompt your SMEs to consider issues relevant to the work of training and the specifics of their contributions by asking these questions:

1. What is most important for this group of learners to know about your area of expertise?
2. What should participants be able to do after hearing and observing your content?
3. Will future salespeople need to know this as well? If so, how would you suggest the knowledge/skill be captured and shared with others?
4. How is this information or skill best delivered—in what setting, by what means, and with what tools and ancillary materials?

The SMEs' answers to these questions help you confirm that you've made a choice of SMEs that fits the training objectives of the business unit—or prompt you to rethink your choice before you've gone so far in the course preparation that you're committed to what you have. The questions help you ensure that content will be delivered in the right venue, to the right people, with the proper training delivery methods because they force the SME to consider all of those aspects of the training.

Noted

An expert is a person who has made all the mistakes which can be made, in a narrow field.

—Niels Bohr, physicist and Nobel laureate

Here are a couple of ideas you can use in coaching an SME to think and behave like an instructor. The first idea involves an SME's favorite pastime. Ask the person to imagine that she is going to train a beginner in some activity or skill she's most passionate about—perhaps windsurfing, scrapbooking, or nature photography. It can be any topic that makes her heart race. When she's picked her topic, have her list the two or three things that are most important for the beginner to know. Ask her to describe what she'd expect the person she's just trained to be able to do on her own. Should the beginner be able to hit the Maui surf confidently? Use the basic scrapbooking tools to capture memories quickly and attractively? Take well-composed photos of a gaggle of geese on a remote lake? Ask her to describe her goal in teaching her hobby to a beginner.

That exercise is a great way to coach someone who doesn't have a background in setting learning objectives. The SME can relate more intimately to the subject matter, she can see how she has to simplify her understanding of the topic to convey it to a beginner, and she can describe in very concrete terms the results she intends to provoke in her trainee. SMEs who are used to doing something rather than explaining what they're doing have to define for themselves what they want to impart before they design their content and the methods for delivering it.

Another way to coach an SME to think like an instructor is to get her to identify the core intent of the training—exactly what kind of action the learner should be able to take when the course is complete. The answers your SME gives to the following six questions will reveal the course objectives:

1. Do the training participants need to **gain knowledge** so they can cite statistics, tabulate numbers, or arrange items in some appropriate order?

2. Do learners need to **comprehend** so they can describe features, tell about benefits, or report results of a sales call?

3. Do they need to **apply what they learn** so they can calculate contingencies or develop a plan for growth in a sales territory?

4. Do participants need to **analyze** so they can detect potential objections or diagram a series of solutions to a problem?

5. Do they need to **synthesize** so they can organize a call itinerary that fits their sales goals for the month, or design a customer event?

6. Do they need to **evaluate** so they can measure close ratios, predict gross sales for the fiscal year, or rank the sales potential of their top five prospects?

Tap into Your SMEs' Expertise to Enhance the Training You Design

Although SMEs don't design training modules or deliver training every day, as you do, they are excellent resources when you're creating a meaningful training event. Even when you're not going to ask them to participate full-throttle in the course design or to deliver the content, you will gain a great deal from partnering with them. From such a partnership, you can

- ▶ get ideas for and feedback on the content of your handouts or other presentation materials
- ▶ get input on developing useful facilitator notes
- ▶ ensure that relevant activities and real-world examples are included in the training.

Here's an example of one Midwest sales training team who chose to engage an SME in content design for an improved ground proximity warning system (GPWS) used in aviation. The company was preparing to launch the improved device and quickly needed to educate the salesforce on its enhanced features and benefits. The training team believed that the content could be delivered best by an expert user from the company's product office. The person chosen was a pilot as well as an expert on the details of the GPWS, so he shared the concerns of the sales reps' target customers—pilots, airline executives, and aviation safety officers. At their second meeting, the SME and the trainer identified the best means of delivering the needed information. They agreed the content didn't require an extensive classroom or webinar presentation; rather, the sales reps would benefit most from a podcast they could carry with them and access whenever they needed to do so. Together, they prepared a script for the podcast and then scheduled a time to record it.

Basic Rule

Having your SMEs record all of their practice sessions in audio or video format will enable them to critique, tweak, and continually evaluate their presentation style privately. If you view some of these practice sessions with them, their confidence will grow as you carefully point out where they excelled and how they can make their delivery even more powerful.

Provide Meaningful Feedback to Your SMEs

Before, during, and after your training, take time to give helpful feedback to your SMEs. Making this an ongoing practice ensures conscientious development of appropriate training and the growth of your SMEs into capable content designers and presenters, and it takes away the burden of anxiety that end-of-session feedback can impart on your nontrainer experts. From the outset until training is finished,

- ▶ tell them what they're doing well
- ▶ explain what would make them even better
- ▶ provide examples of their content or delivery style that should be refined or continued.

When you've engaged several SMEs to assist with a course, plan a time to meet with them as a group when the training is complete. This opens a space for them to give feedback to one another and to you. Remember that feedback sessions must be made safe, comfortable, and nonthreatening. Try a roundtable discussion. Each SME starts by sharing what he liked about the presentation and what could be done differently. Give your insights at the end. Offering opportunities for ongoing feedback is crucial if you want the quality of training to continue to improve.

One Final Note About Using SMEs

Throughout this chapter, we've explored how significant SME engagement can be to the outcome of your training. Not only do SMEs increase the value you take to your stakeholders and training participants, they also help you generate more training buy-in throughout the organization. Your SMEs are walking billboards for your sales training, and they help market and brand your program. Partnering with resident experts is an opportunity you won't want to miss. The long-term benefits are worth every minute you invest in developing your SMEs.

Getting It Done

Give your SMEs the following checklist as a tool to help them design their sessions:

☐ I have developed learning objectives.

☐ I have met with the stakeholders to learn valuable information about my audience.

☐ I have brainstormed
    a. main ideas
    b. subsequent ideas.

☐ I know what I will use to support my content:
    a. handouts
    b. visuals
    c. activities
    d. discussions.

☐ I have conveyed the benefits of what I am delivering.

☐ I have a powerful and memorable
    a. introduction/opening
    b. conclusion.

11

Developing a
Sales Training Brand

Michelle M. Harrison

■■

What's Inside This Chapter

In this chapter, you'll learn

▶ The importance of building a sales training brand strategy
▶ How to create a sales training brand
▶ How to create your sales training marketing strategy.

In the early American west, cattle rustling was a crime that was punished severely, with hangings rather uncommon. To thwart thieves, or at least make it possible to identify stolen cattle and return them to their herds, ranchers created brands. These simple images also acted as trademarks and came to represent pride of ownership among cattlemen.

Over time, commercial industries began using the term "brand" to mean the qualities, characteristics, and practices that made them unique. They developed "brand names" for their specific products and services to set them apart from other similar market entries, to help them build their businesses, and to increase sales and customer loyalty.

Cows aside, a brand today is more than a logo or a distinctive typeface and color palette. It's the story or message or full experience surrounding a product, service, or company. A brand goes beyond the details to target a consumer's emotions. Essentially, a brand is the way that a buyer or user "feels" when she tries the product or when he uses the service. For example, Miller Brewing Company describes Miller Lite with the phrase "Tastes Great, Less Filling!" FedEx defines its shipping service as "Absolutely Overnight." Those two simple phrases tell consumers what distinguishes the product and the service from other available choices. If a picture is worth a thousand words, a recognizable brand is worth pictures and words and attitudes and sensory input and experiences—it's more than words can say and pictures can show in a tiny moment of time. It's all that and more.

Companies spend millions creating and conveying brand messages that will drive customer loyalty. Consider the 2009 Super Bowl. Advertisers spent a record-breaking average of $3 million for a 30-second TV spot to put their brand message on what's considered the most widely watched television event of the year.

The Importance of Branding Your Sales Training

As sales, learning, and performance professionals, you teach others to sell your company, your products or services, and your company brand. You spend countless hours conducting research, developing sales training materials, and delivering top-quality courses, all while continuing to gain product knowledge and identify training trends that support what you do. But do you spend time and effort developing a brand strategy for your sales training department?

For sales trainers, it's important to define your course offerings and get out the message of your training department. How do you want people to feel about your department? In what way do you want your department to be known? Creating and

Basic Rule
Take every opportunity to showcase your sales training. Find ways to deliver your brand message in any likely venue—even in casual conversation.

Noted

Your premium brand had better be delivering something special, or it's not going to get the business.

—Warren Buffett, American investment entrepreneur

conveying a clear brand image is the best way to define yourselves in your own terms before anyone on the outside does it for you.

Branding what you do, what you stand for, and how you contribute to your organization's bottom line is imperative in establishing the worth and credibility of your training department. You need your audience quickly to identify what you can do for them. Investing time and resources in developing a way to articulate who you are and what you offer helps focus your team on its vital work, and the resulting brand shows your stakeholders and prospective learners what your department offers and how they can benefit from it.

Editor's Notebook

Every time I speak to a group about my team, I share the same story: We're a team of passionate and creative sales learning and performance instructors. We create solutions that help drive revenue and increase customer retention for our salesforce. This story is our brand promise—one we deliver on 100 percent of the time.

A message like the one in the Editor's Notebook helps the organization's salespeople recognize that your training team is serious about your company's goals and strategies. It conveys the fact that we're in it together—sales reps and sales trainers alike.

Senior leaders typically measure company success by evaluating analytics, sales numbers, and the company's return on investment. They expect the same from our training departments. Although proving return-on-investment can be a challenge in a training department where returns depend on the post-training actions of others, creating a strong and positive brand for your department describes your value, adds visibility, and keeps you in decision makers' sight lines.

Crafting and Conveying Your Brand Image

There are several steps in creating a department brand and using it to your greatest advantage in communicating value and selling your services to management stakeholders and learners. Here are those steps in brief:

▶ Search the soul of your department to identify its value to the organization.

▶ Develop an image that most closely portrays that value and simplify it into a unique and recognizable brand.

▶ Create marketing materials that convey the brand consistently.

▶ Plan and carry out a campaign to get your brand into the organizational marketplace.

▶ Reinforce the brand with ongoing communication strategies.

▶ Monitor response to your brand over time and make needed modifications to remain current.

Identify Your Department's Value

Have you ever made a purchase and then thought, That was a great value? If so, what did you mean? For example, if you're buying a new car, the value to you might be engine performance, but the value to someone else might be convenience and comfort of the interior options selected. The perception of "value" is very subjective and individual. To determine the value of your department, you have to identify its immediate benefits for your training participants and stakeholders.

The most important factor to define is why a leader should invest the time, budget, and effort in sending her or his salespeople to your training. When the sales reps receive training from your team, what do the leader, the business unit, and the organization gain? Your sales training team is crucial to the organization and its bottom line, but you have to be able to articulate why and how that's true.

For example, our team is passionate and creative in finding and devising training solutions that equip our sales reps to drive results, to help customers grow their businesses, and to increase revenue. Each of us believes that the more our team knows, the more the company will grow—in knowledge, in skill, and in finances. By providing sales skills, product knowledge, and technical know-how, we prepare our salespeople to hit the ground running faster than reps who haven't attended our training. This is the value our team brings to the organization.

So, how about you? Think about what makes you, your training team, and your department valuable assets to the organization. Start by answering these questions:

1. What is the goal of your department? What do you want to accomplish? Is it to make it easy for your salesforce to gain knowledge? Or do you have a target number associated with your goal—perhaps growing the number of sales in a particular area by *x* amount? (Whatever your goal, advertise it and use it in your brand messaging.)

2. What nouns and adjectives describe your training department? (During my course on personal branding, I ask participants to make a list of terms that describe them, that define their brand promise or the value they take to their customers. You should do the same thing. Are you and your team *creative, trustworthy, resourceful, fun*? Are you *experts in your field, troubleshooters, partners, advisers*? List them all, and be thorough. Ask your previous participants, stakeholders, and anyone you've worked with in the past, too. This exercise will truly help build your training brand.)

3. What are the goals of your salesforce? And how can you affect those goals most significantly?

4. What courses or topics have helped former participants sell more? (If you don't know, ask them.)

5. Who has had success after attending one or more of your courses? (Reach out to them for a testimonial.)

Develop a Simple and Unique Brand

Just as cattle brands don't have intricate details because they've got to be readable on the run and at a distance, your brand shouldn't have lots of ruffles and flourishes. Too much fluff or too much data masks the real message your brand is trying to impart. Make it simple and uniquely representative of the sales training department. Here are some questions to get you thinking about a meaningful and simple image:

1. What kind of impact do you want to make on your organization?
2. What do your sales reps need?
3. What benefits do you offer to salespeople who take your courses?
4. In what ways will your courses help salespeople improve their performance?
5. For what traits and characteristics do you want your team to be known?
6. What is unique about your department? About your approach to training? About your courses?

Your answers to all of those questions begin to define your brand. When you've answered them, it's time to evaluate your value and branding questions. You can't be everything to everyone, so you've got to whittle down your lists to just a few things for which you and your department want to be known. For example, FedEx does a lot of things right, but their brand promise and the value they sell—the one you see on every advertisement—is that they guarantee your package will reach its destination "absolutely overnight."

What do your department and company want to achieve as a result of your training? Improved sales results? Thorough product knowledge? A sales staff that's more efficient and better informed? Consistency? Innovation? Responsiveness? You now must truly search your team's soul and find those things for which you want to be known. To do that, take the answers to all of the questions you have asked yourself and begin to identify only those items for which you want to be—or for which you already are—known.

Let's use a case study to illustrate the branding process. Julie is a training manager for a large window manufacturing company. The salespeople are responsible for selling the company's windows to building supply stores across the country. One of the goals of the sales team is to increase the amount of sales from each of its storefronts by 20 percent this year. When Julie and her team asked the questions above, this is what she found:

1. The goals of the sales training team were to educate the salesforce on product knowledge and to keep them informed of new technology, product enhancements, and alerts.
2. Some of the adjectives she heard repeated for her department were *quick, responsive, experts in knowledge of our product, conscientious,* and *respectful of the sales representative's time.*
3. Julie and her team wanted to establish a tie to the revenue return that the company would realize as a result of increased sales of their newest eco-friendly windows. They also wanted to contribute to the number of sales visits the sales reps made.
4. The sales reps needed quick-hit information when they reached the field, but when they were new in their positions, they needed excellent new-hire training programs designed to fill their specific needs as new employees and relevant sales training that covered product knowledge and selling skills.

5. Julie and her team went through participant evaluations gathered over the past four years, and they found that, above all else, Julie's team helped sales reps better manage their time and did an excellent job in equipping new hires with the knowledge and skill they needed to hit their sales quotas.

6. Julie then evaluated and compared the sales performance of those who had attended training and those who had not. She was thrilled to find that, on average, those who attended training were 20 percent more productive than those who had not attended.

7. Julie and her team wanted to be known for their just-in-time training and their quick and thorough tips for selling new features and products. Most important, they wanted to be seen as a team that could help the group save time and increase sales by improving its processes to complete tasks.

8. Out of all the things that are different about Julie's team, the most unique aspect is that they've found innovative ways to reach reps in the field through social media, blogs, and podcasts—thereby being even more efficient and timely in getting new material to the salesforce. They made it simple to learn.

From all that they learned, Julie and the training team created this brand: "We help our sales team meet its goals by designing innovative and meaningful product training that puts the knowledge and tools in our salespeople's hands faster and more easily."

Create Marketing Materials That Are Recognizable and Consistent

Your brand, conveyed in the materials and media you use to market your courses, is like your business attire and your aftershave—it's the first impression you make and what lingers when you leave. A polished and professional appearance put together with care suggests that you apply the same attention to your performance. The marketing materials you present do the same thing—they stand in for you and your team, revealing your brand and describing your work. If your team looks professional and your training courses get rave reviews, but your marketing materials are just mediocre, you've lost the chance to present a total package that's professional, believable, and trustworthy. The materials you create have to appeal to and draw in the reader. The materials have a very significant impact on how he or she views you.

The design you choose also should reflect the personality of your team. For example, if you're a sales team who supports training for a mortgage company, your materials probably will be more formal and professional. If you support the sales training for a chain of Internet cafes, you might have a more relaxed, hip design.

When designing your marketing materials, think about what is most important to the customer and make that your headline. The most important data should come first, followed by supporting information that showcases your department. It has to be user-friendly, too. Think about the flow of your material. Does it read well, and is the content organized in an order that helps the reader understand it?

Design and color are also vital factors. Determine your color scheme and again consider your team's personality. Make that color scheme evident on every piece of electronic, paper, and web content you put out for view. The more your audience sees these, the more you build brand awareness for your team.

And, most important, always include your value proposition and/or tagline on every marketing piece you create. Again, the more customers see it, hear it, and experience it, the stronger your brand identification will be.

If your training department already has marketing materials, try this exercise to test their effectiveness. Gather every pamphlet, curriculum description, training manual, binder cover, class handout, screen shots of all your training webpages, and examples of any other materials associated with your department. Lay them out on a large table and then answer the following questions about what you see:

1. Is the look unique and distinct from other departments' materials, or does it remind you of something you've seen before?
2. Are the look and feel consistent across all the materials?
3. Is a message clearly conveyed?
4. Are the logo, major typefaces, and color scheme the same on all of the items?

Think About This

You never get a second chance to make a first impression. Take the time to create polished, professional materials. Cutting corners to save a little money always produces a second-rate product and is sure to cost you more in the long run.

Be consistent, thorough, and diligent in ensuring consistency of appearance across your entire marketing array, both in print and electronic. When someone sees your material, he or she should think immediately of your sales training and the distinct benefits it offers.

Get Your Brand Out There: Plan and Implement a Marketing Campaign

When you feel confident about what you can do for your organization and your salespeople, and when you have a strong brand image in place, it's time to begin a branding campaign. Your goal is to educate the organization about your department brand, your training team, and the resources you provide. If you aren't explaining where you stand, others are left to create their own version of what your team does.

This educating process can be done in a variety of ways. Your methods will depend on the size of your organization, its culture, and your resources. Here are some ideas:

- ▶ Hold a meeting with the chief executive officer and her direct reports to start the message trickling down. One way to accomplish this is to ask your CEO to host a celebratory event to unveil your brand. It's a unique way to show executive support and create a stir about your brand.
- ▶ Publish a series of articles in your company newsletter or on its website. These should be geared toward what is important to your sales team. The articles might offer selling tips, ideas for overcoming buyer objections, general information or company positions on hot topics in the field, competitor comparisons, or recognition of top salespeople.
- ▶ Send an email to all employees. The message might be a simple update on your last graduating class, news about upcoming training opportunities, awards your department has received, or a "did-you-know?" note. The point is to be visible often—without being too annoying.
- ▶ Prepare a podcast. It's a fantastic way to swiftly get sales and product information to the reps in the field, and it offers easy access for your sales team.
- ▶ During your classes (whether live, via the web, or through teleconferencing) provide an overview of the resources your training team offers. Take a small amount of time to explain to or remind participants where they can find the helpful tools your team provides. No one will know how to get ahold of all these great sales aids if you don't tell them.

Each organization has its own preferred way of communicating internally. Be diligent in exploring and using whatever means will reach your audience most effectively.

In preparing a campaign to get your message out, a marketing plan is your map to success. To develop a plan you'll define your campaign goals and milestones and identify ways to achieve them.

Because poor planning produces a range of problems, find someone in your department who will be accountable for the marketing plan. Involve this person early on when the plan is first being imagined and created, and encourage his or her personal ownership all the way through implementation.

The plan can take one of many different formats, based on the industry or personality of your department. No matter what format you choose, these are the elements you must include in your marketing plan:

- **Mission statement**—This is a clear and brief description of the overall mission and goal of your training department.
    - What are your goals, and what do you want to accomplish?
    - For what do you want your training department to be known?

- **Specific goals and deadlines**—These are concrete, measurable goals with a timetable attached.
    - What is your training department's first priority?
    - What potential problems could confound your goals or upset your schedule?

- **Pulse checks**—These are points when you stop and assess your plan.
    - Is the marketing plan working for you? Have you justified the investment of time and resources in developing your marketing materials? Has the plan increased the perceived value of what your team offers?
    - If the plan is not working, when do you stop and adjust? At what point is a major change needed?

- **Future goals and next steps**—This is a bullet list of additional desired outcomes and action items to continue successfully marketing your sales training.

- ▶ How do you ensure that marketing continues to occur?
- ▶ What are your big goals over the next five years?
- ▶ How will you stay on top of implementing, monitoring, and sustaining your marketing plan?

Here are some tips for building your plan:

- ▶ **Take a first step.** Get your team together and draft your mission statement; then build from there. Often the biggest roadblock to creating your marketing plan is making that first step. Take on your plan in manageable chunks. Remember, you can't do it all at one time.
- ▶ **Honor the power of brainstorming.** In brainstorming sessions, random thoughts turn into great ideas. Hold sessions often with your team and encourage them to go all out.
- ▶ **Give yourself options.** There always are multiple ways to achieve the same goal, so don't discount an idea because it isn't the usual way of doing something or because your competition isn't doing it that way. Make sure to have a plan B.
- ▶ **Establish metrics to gauge the outcomes.** How else can you tell if what you're doing is working the way you intend it to? With more and more pressure to make sure we're spending our dollars wisely, measurement is something we must do. And don't underestimate some side-effect values to your marketing efforts. For example, if one goal is to create an e-newsletter about your course offerings and dates, a side-effect resulting from that newsletter would be heightened awareness and increased enrollment in your sessions. Count those as measurable effects when you're setting metrics.
- ▶ **Keep every idea.** In sum or part, ideas that don't fit today may make more sense to us at a different time. Keep an idea journal that you can refer to on days when you need to jump-start your creativity. One sales training team keeps a file folder for every idea or initiative that was brought to them, including details on who posed the idea and any supporting documents and research. When time allows or the idea enhances another project that's in the works, the team pulls the file and implements the idea.
- ▶ **Use technology.** Technology enables us to do many things with little or no effort. Through the electronic gadgetry in our personal lives, we constantly are being made aware of offers and opportunities. Translate that passion for

immediacy and connection to the work world, too. If currently you don't feel comfortable with MySpace, Facebook, Twitter, LinkedIn, or iPhones, start using those technologies. Their popularity is expanding every day, new uses are emerging, and their future use is all but guaranteed. Using these technologies will give you incredible resources to help you create and execute your marketing plan.

▶ **Target your message and style the content to fit the audience.** Don't just mass-mail information to a broad audience. Use data to find a better target that's more likely to yield positive results. If you're reaching out to more than one audience, adjust your messages to suit the recipients. If you're targeting upper management, your communication should be more structured and direct: just the facts. If targeting call center associates, your communication should be attractive and fun to read. Better to craft two communications and reach both groups of people than to rely on one and miss both marks.

▶ **Nail your first impression.** Try out your brand on people who will give you honest feedback before you start marketing to your most important group.

Regardless of its size and scope, your marketing plan should remain a working document that you repeatedly review and refine. Waiting for mistakes to happen wastes time and causes your team to lose focus. Stay proactive and continually assess your plan and your progress.

Reinforce Your Brand with Ongoing Communication Strategies

When you complete your campaign, make the information you shared easily accessible to anyone who hears about your department and programs. Continued reminders and a communication plan are essential in extending and capitalizing on your brand identity.

Stay Current: Monitor Response and Refresh the Brand When Needed

Think about a well-respected company that you know. What comes to mind about that company? Chances are it's the visual representation of the organization: the logo, the tagline, the colors, and so forth. For Wal-Mart it's blue; for Starbucks it's the "green mermaid"; for Shell Oil it's the shell. These are the organizations' brands. And the brands make the organizations recognizable and tangible. The same holds true for your department's brand. Don't stop when the rollout is complete or after you've implemented your marketing strategy. Rather, assign someone on your team to monitor your brand image over the long term.

This monitoring includes continual surveys of your stakeholders and learners, and assessments of their impressions of your team and your course offerings. By surveying your participants and other stakeholders, you'll learn

▶ why, when, and how they choose to attend your training events
▶ if they feel you deliver on your brand promises
▶ how your marketing dollars are paying off (for example, whether you're seeing increased results in attendance figures).

This valuable information lets you know if your brand is resonating with key members of the organization. If you discover that it's not, you can use the information to tweak or update the brand so that it's more effective. Feedback also will identify less successful aspects of your training programs. The earlier you discover a dip in brand resonance or a way to improve the product you're delivering, the better.

Basic Rule

Always start your marketing strategy with a mission statement. This is your road map to everything else you do.

More Tips for Successful Branding

To help your organization stand out in the minds of your sales team, you should create a branding plan that covers the following:

▶ Be prepared to state what your brand is within a 30-second timeframe. This is what's called the "elevator speech"—a synopsis you could give in a ride between floors. You never know when you might have an opportunity to advertise. Here's an example: "It's my passion to provide creative sales training solutions to help your sales team grow and meet your territory goals. In today's environment, getting more from your sales teams is essential to the company's success. My team and I develop sales education that drives results, increases retention, and ultimately helps your salesforce meet its goals. Think of us as an extension to your region. I'd love the chance to discuss how we can influence your strategic plan. What day next week works best for you?"

▶ Find someone credible in your industry to give a testimonial about your brand. Use this in marketing on posters and flyers, in newspapers, radio ads, direct mail pieces, and postcards.

▶ Find unique times to hit your target market. When would your brand be needed? When do departments need training? Immediately after hiring new people? Thirty to 60 days after that? When do your clients put their budgets together? These questions can help you narrow your search.

▶ Always think creatively when identifying places to market. For example, during its "Ask Chuck" ad campaign, Charles Schwab advertised on airline sick sacks. Very clever. Can you use vending machine areas, break rooms, the cafeteria, or even the restrooms to highlight your brand?

▶ Design your graphics so they work well in both black and white and color, depending on your need. This will save you time and money under short deadlines.

▶ Remember this: When it comes to verbiage, less is more. You don't need to tell them everything up front. Make them want to know more, but include a call to action so they know how to get more. Do you have a unique phone extension or even your own web address?

▶ Research and know any legal guidelines or regulations that may apply when promoting your training work.

▶ Negotiate or barter for publicity. Ask for discounts, or try to exchange services. If you don't ask, chances are you won't get it. There always are "free" ways to get publicity. Try investigating some of these ideas in your network: newsletters, bulletin boards, professional associations, or conferences.

▶ Be timeless in your message and your graphics. Avoid anything too trendy or gimmicky.

▶ Look at others' success. Can you remember brands that were introduced five years ago? Are they still advertising today? What key elements made them successful or memorable? What specific details stand out for you now?

■ ■ ■

Throughout this chapter you've discovered the value in branding and marketing what you offer. It's an integral part of your business. Your sales teams won't remember what you offer or how it creates value for them in the field unless you continuously keep the information in front of their eyes and inside their ears. Take the time to create your marketing plan.

Think About This

Create a way to reveal only a portion of your brand as a teaser. Get your audience interested, create a draw, and then give them the whole story. One group emails a Tip of the Week. Here's an example of one such message: "Looking for new ways to prospect? We promise to save you time in cultivating leads. Check out our website to learn more." This email showcases their brand (time savings) for the salesforce, and it entices readers to visit the group's website. The site's splash page takes them to a full list of training resources, including the department's entire brand message.

Getting It Done

You can gather a wealth of information through surveys, focus groups, or meetings. The process you select isn't as important as the feedback you get, so do something. Here are some questions to elicit answers that help you enhance your brand message:

1. What do you like about our department?
2. What do you dislike about our department?
3. How do you feel about our department and the resources/classes we provide?
4. Do you believe in and trust our department?
5. Can you explain what our department can do for you?
6. When you hear about our department, what are your first few thoughts?

For most people, interpreting a brand is like trying to read hieroglyphics. But like any language, brands become readable with experience and understanding. Don't let your department, your team, or the resources you provide be viewed as a hieroglyph in the world of sales training. Make it clear and put it out there repeatedly so people recognize and relate to it.

Conclusion

■ ■

Baltimore Oriole Cal Ripken Jr. once said, "Play every game as if it were the most important game of the season." That's advice we must all take. Remember that every session you deliver is your most important one. You have the opportunity and the challenge to teach salespeople—a unique audience. To be great working with them, you have to bring your A-game 100 percent of the time to keep them engaged, invested, and on their toes.

Think like a salesperson, provide above-and-beyond service, and present sales-issue solutions for the greater good of the company.

Throughout this book, you've learned to apply to your own sales training program some of the same basic sales skills you teach your sales reps. For example, you've applied your skills in marketing to promote your classes and build your personal brand. You've learned how assessing your participants' personalities can help you win them over in the learning environment and keep them engaged in class— just as you teach your sales teams to assess their customers' and prospects' personalities. When you help your trainees transfer what they've learned into what they do in the field, you've essentially closed the sale of your program's worth and begun to maintain a future relationship with your sales team.

Ultimately, the information offered here is only as good as the use you make of it. To put the material to work in a way that's meaningful for you, your training team, your learners, and your organization, follow these few important steps:

1. Establish one or two goals or actions you want to implement in your training.
2. Go back and complete the exercises and questions at the chapter ends ("Getting It Done").

3. Set milestones for yourself and your training team to ensure you're meeting your goals.

You have the knowledge and skills necessary to be even more effective in delivering training to your salesforce. And you've gathered valuable strategies that can help you sell your training programs to key stakeholders in the company. Use those strategies to your advantage. Teach every class as if it were your very first and your most important session. Then you'll be most likely to change the minds of those salespeople who feel time away from the field is wasted. People who would rather be selling than learning—the impatient learners—will be knocking on your office door begging to be a part of your learning environment.

Resources

■■

Books and Articles

Akpinar, Burhan. 2005. "The Role of Sense of Smell in Learning and the Effects of Aroma in Cognitive Learning." *Pakistan Journal of Social Science* 3(7): 952–60.

Bloom, Benjamin S., ed. 1956. *Taxonomy of Educational Objectives: Handbook 1: Cognitive Domain.* New York: Longman.

Forman, David C. 2003. "Eleven Common-Sense Learning Principles: Lessons from Experience, Sages, and Each Other." *T+D* September.

HR Chally Group. 2007. "The 2007 Chally World Class Sales Excellence Research Report: The Route to the Summit." Available at http://www.chally.com.

Lambert, Brian W. *10 Steps to Successful Sales.* Alexandria, VA: ASTD Press.

Lambert, Brian W., Tim Ohai, and Eric M. Kerkhoff. 2009. *World-Class Selling: New Sales Competencies.* Alexandria, VA: ASTD Press.

Phillips, Jack J. 2003. *Return on Investment in Training and Performance Improvement Programs*, second edition. Boston: Butterworth-Heinemann.

Yorton, Tom. 2003. "Improv-Based Training: It's Not Just Fun and Games." *T+D* September.

Internet Resources

Integrity Solutions, http://www.integritysolutions.com. *In addition to white papers, Integrity has an array of resources available to sales trainers.*

New Horizons for Learning, http://www.Newhorizons.org/strategies/arts/brewer.htm. *Learn more about integrating music in your training sessions.*

Marcia L. Conner, Ageless Learner, http://www.agelesslearner.com/assess/learningstyle.html. *This is a quick assessment of learning styles that helps you get to know your audience faster.*

Sense of Smell Institute, http://www.senseofsmell.org. *Find out more about the influences of scents in your classes.*

Webinars and Synchronous Learning

Fugent, http://www.fugent.com. *This hosting site uses the WebEx platform.*

GoToMeeting, www.gotomeeting.com. *This hosting site enables easy virtual meetings, sales presentations, and online training.*

Computer-Based Training Development Tools

Articulate, http://www.articulate.com. *Developers of e-learning software and authoring tools.*

Trivantis Corporation, http://www.trivantis.com. *This firm's e-learning software, called Lectora, is a rather advanced tool with a steeper learning curve than Articulate's software. It's for experienced users and offers great flexibility.*

Mobile Content

Wimob, http://www.wimob.com. *Free technology that lets you download multimedia content from any website to a mobile phone.*

Wikis

Wikipatterns, http://www.wikipatterns.com. *Here you'll learn how to create support for a wiki in your organization or group.*

Wikispaces, http://www.wikispaces.com. *This site offers free and upgraded wiki accounts. Discussion boards are included as well.*

Discussion Boards

Blackboard, http://www.blackboard.com. *This is a discussion board site for educational purposes.*

Blogs and Podcasting

Blog Catalog, http://www.blogcatalog.com. *This free site directs you to a vast array of blogs on thousands of topics.*

Blogger, http://www.blogger.com. *Create and post your blog on this free site.*

BlogSpot, http://www.blogspot.com. *Use this free site to create your own blog.*

iLife, http://www.itunes.com. *For Mac platforms, this site offers a podcasting tool.*

About the Editor

Angela Siegfried, CPLP, AIP, has more than 16 years' experience in leadership development and adult education. She has led students in a variety of learning experiences within the airline and insurance industries and in not-for-profit organizations. Siegfried has designed, developed, and delivered training for executives, managers, and associates in technical, soft skills, and sales arenas. She is the director of sales learning and performance for Allied Insurance, a member of Nationwide Insurance. Her primary responsibilities there include consulting with internal sales associates and independent agents to create and present educational offerings that help salespeople meet their business goals.

Siegfried is an active member of the local and national chapters of the American Society for Training & Development and is past president of central Iowa ASTD. She has served on the board as vice president of programming, as committee chair for the Iowa Character Counts in Business initiative, and as vice president of community relations. During her time on the board, Siegfried has worked with ASTD teams to develop alliances with community organizations, create marketing and promotional strategies, and develop philanthropic partnerships with the business community in central Iowa.

Siegfried and her husband Aaron are the proud parents of three very active children. In addition to experiencing life through her children's eyes, she enjoys scrapbooking, camping, traveling, gardening, interior decorating, and shopping for bargains.

She can be reached at aarringdale@aol.com or 515.371.5524.

About the Contributors

■ ■

Carol A. Dawson

Carol A. Dawson, MS, CPCU, CPLP, CIC, CISR, AIS, is a learning and performance consultant for Nationwide Insurance in Des Moines, Iowa. She graduated from MidAmerica Nazarene College (now University) in Olathe, Kansas, with a major in Communications/Public Relations and Psychology. Her first job out of college was in the personal lines service center at Allied Insurance. Since then she has held positions as an agent and an underwriter, but found her passion in learning and performance. She enjoys volunteering, currently serving as vice president of communication for the Central Iowa ASTD chapter and is actively involved in Toastmasters, having served as president from 2006-2008. She is also an adult Sunday School teacher and local missionary president. She completed her master's degree in Adult Learning and Organizational Performance at Drake University in Des Moines, Iowa.

Michelle M. Harrison

Michelle M. Harrison is a marketing consultant for a large insurance company. She graduated from Iowa State University where she majored in journalism and mass communications. With more than 20 years experience in several major corporations geared toward customer service and the marketplace, she has enjoyed finding new and innovative ways to make the components of communication, advertising, public relations, marketing, training, and strategy all work together. She and her husband enjoy spending time with their two young sons in Des Moines, Iowa.

Brian W. Lambert

Brian W. Lambert, PhD, is the director of ASTD's Sales Training Drivers, where he works with internal and external clients and ASTD members to create relevant content, tools, and resources for sales trainers, sales managers, and senior executives. Lambert manages ASTD's sales competency modeling and sales training research and is a highly sought after expert on delivering sales training, managing and developing high-performing sales talent, and improving salesperson performance.

Lambert has 15 years of experience in all aspects of sales, sales management, and sales training. Before joining ASTD, he founded the United Professional Sales Association, where he oversaw the development of standards for salesperson performance worldwide. His work on salesperson competencies has helped thousands of sales team members around the world measure themselves against the standards of world-class selling. In 2006, Lambert was recognized by Sales & Marketing Management as one of the most influential people in professional selling. He has a bachelor's degree from the University of Central Florida, a master's of science degree in Administration and Human Resource Management from Central Michigan University, and a PhD from Capella University.

Renie McClay

Renie McClay has managed training for three *Fortune* 500 companies. Her sales career started with Kraft in sales, account management, and sales management which led to a passion for learning and development. She has hired sales teams and sales trainers. Her company, Inspired Learning LLC, helps organizations design and deliver programs and curriculum globally. She brings creativity and innovation to all she does, being certified in accelerated innovation with Solution People and in improvisation with Second City. McClay is past president of SMT: Center for Sales Excellence. She is the author of *10 Steps to Successful Teams* (ASTD, 2009), *Fortify Your Sales Force: Leading and Training Strong Teams, The Essential Guide to Training Global Audiences,* and *Sales Training Solutions.*

Tim Ohai

Tim Ohai is founder and president of Growth & Associates, a consulting association that focuses on the people dynamics of change, both organizationally and personally. Growth & Associates has created fit-for-purpose solutions for companies in a variety of industries, including ASTD, Shell Oil, and Wal-Mart. With more than a decade of learning and development experience, Ohai brings a rare combination of high energy and real-life savvy to consult on large, complex strategic issues, especially around the topics of key customer strategies, alignment, and organizational change. Ohai's areas of expertise include sales performance, executive coaching, and developing the talent pipeline for emerging generations, but he also consults on key customer strategies, alignment, and organizational change. He has been recognized as a global coaching and sales expert, and his expertise has taken him to Latin America, Europe, Africa, Asia, and the Middle East.

Paul Smith

Paul Smith has worked in the fields of education and workplace learning and performance for more than 18 years. He has designed, implemented, evaluated, and delivered instruction to almost every age group, career level, and learning style. He has achieved professional success in the fields of sales, journalism, and education, and he has led change initiatives in civic, corporate, and political arenas. Currently, Smith is a senior training analyst with the Principal Financial Group, where he also serves on the corporate-level Development Council. He also serves as the Children's Ministries director for LifePointe Church in Ames, Iowa. He is a registered representative with Princor Financial. Smith served his local ASTD chapter as vice president of finance and board president and currently serves in the newly launched position of vice president of strategic partnerships. He has also served as chairperson of ASTD National's Chapter Recognition Committee and as an ASTD National Adviser for Chapters.

Index